From Ministry
to Theology

From Ministry to Theology

Pastoral Action & Reflection

John Patton

All meaningful knowledge is for the sake of action, and all meaningful action is for the sake of friendship.

THE SELF AS AGENT
John Macmurray

Abingdon Press
Nashville

FROM MINISTRY TO THEOLOGY
PASTORAL ACTION AND REFLECTION

Library of Congress Cataloging-in-Publication Data

Patton, John, 1930-
 From ministry to theology : pastoral action and reflection / John Patton.
  p.   cm.
 Includes bibliographical references.
 ISBN 0-687-13654-7 (alk. paper)
 1. Pastoral theology. 2. Experience (Religion) 3. Imagination-Religious aspects—Christianity. 4. Pastoral psychology—Study and teaching. 5. Theology—Methodology. I. Title.
 BV4011.P385   1990
 253'.01—dc20   90-40426
                                                  CIP

Scripture quotations in this publication are from the Revised Standard Version of the Bible, copyright 1946, 1952, 1971 by the Division of Christian Education of the National Council of the Churches of Christ in the USA, and are used by permission.

The epilogue was adapted from John Patton, "Pastoral Supervision and Theology," *Journal of Supervision and Training in Ministry* 8 (1986). Used by permission.

The dialogue and text involving "Elise" on pages 81-84 is adapted from John Patton, "Toward a Theology of Pastoral Event: Reflections on the work of Seward Hiltner," *The Journal of Pastoral Care* 40 (June 1986). Used by permission.

MANUFACTURED IN THE UNITED STATES OF AMERICA

To
C. Benton Kline
colleague and friend
who has contributed
to many books
written by others

Acknowledgments

I acknowledge my indebtedness to the many groups of CPE students, seminary students, and some lay pastoral care groups in local churches who have helped me to formulate these ideas by sharing some of their "meaning-full" events. I am appreciative of my CPE supervisor colleagues, Bill Boyle, J. D. Chelette, Zeke Delozier, Kerry Duncan, Ross Hightower, and Eugene Robinson who, each year for over fifteen years, encouraged me in conducting a theological reflection seminar with their students. Ben Kline, to whom this book is dedicated, and Brian Childs, colleagues at Columbia Seminary, have again been helpful with their suggestions and critiques. David Pacini, a faculty colleague at the Candler School of Theology at Emory University, was an active participant and theological consultant in several of the groups. Seminars with CPE supervisors and pastors in a number of places provided opportunities to formulate many of the ideas in the book. Most important, Helen, my wife, has helpfully criticized what I have written. She continues to share imaginatively in the action, relationships, and meaning in my life.

Contents

Prologue

"I don't have it written down," said Doug, "but I'll never forget it." The group of chaplain residents in our clinical pastoral education center had been asked to present a pastoral event that seemed to be full of meaning and in some way evocative of theological reflection. The event that Doug shared involved a baby who had been stillborn. The parents wanted to have a memorial service in the hospital chapel. Doug tried in vain to get a more experienced chaplain to officiate at the service because he felt he did not know what to do.

When he found that he would need to do the service himself, he quickly prepared some things to say. However, when the nurse brought the stillborn baby into the chapel where he and the parents were, Doug found that he could not say what he had planned to say. "All I could do was stand there and cry." Not knowing what to expect, Doug was not surprised when the nurse handed him the baby to hold. "I want you to baptize my baby," the mother said. "Her name is Nicole." Doug nodded, but he saw no water with which to baptize the baby. Almost without thinking he took a tissue, wiped the tears from the eyes of the parents and his own eyes, and touched it to the baby's head and whispered, "Nicole, I baptize you in the name of the Father, Son and Holy Ghost. Amen."[1]

One can immediately see how this event is "meaning-full," and how it might have influenced Doug's understanding of himself, his ministry, and his theology. Even so, it might not have had this influence unless something had been done with it. It might easily have been lost, with Doug remembering only that he had a significant clinical experience in the hospital. I am convinced, as was Doug, that the event needed to be claimed to enrich both Doug's future practice of ministry and his understanding of Christian faith.

What happened to Doug doesn't happen every day. We may be tempted to contrast it with our own experience, which we dismiss because such drama seldom occurs in our lives. Although the events of our lives may be less dramatic, it is more likely that we fail to recognize experiences that are potentially "meaning-full" because we do not have an adequate method and context for dealing with them. Christian ministry involves not only understanding what we do in the light of our faith, but also understanding our faith in the light of what we do. Thus this book calls for the recovery of and respect for our experience, particularly our experience as pastors, and describes a way of "talking back" to our faith in the light of the "meaning-full" events of our lives. The vitality of congregations in the future depends on theological students, ordained clergy, and laity who are exploring the ways that we can move from event to theology, who are discovering how events that seem to be "meaning-full" can be re-created, shared, and appropriated for the ministry of Christ.

Although theological reflection on pastoral practice is important, there may be considerable resistance to doing it. It may be dismissed as either unimportant or too difficult for the average person, something in which only professional theologians spend time. Members of lay ministry groups in congregations often resist in one way or another. "The important thing is getting the job done, seeing the new membership prospects or the shut-ins. Theological thinking takes too much time and is really a job for the clergy." Variations on this theme come from supervisors of clinical pastoral education programs who are very much aware that their funding comes from students doing ministry, not theology. Certainly, the job *is* important, more important than thinking about it, and the only effective counter to this resistance is demonstrating that theological reflection can contribute to a more effective and purposeful ministry.

When relating practice to theology or, particularly, when developing a method or a training program for reflection, some experts may also dismiss the work as unimportant because it is too easy and, therefore, needs no particular time or attention devoted to it. "Why do we need to bother with all this," the argument goes. "The theological meaning of these experiences is obvious." Persons who take this point of view usually present themselves as comfortable with religious words. They tend to assume that the way they have learned to talk about their experiences in a Christian manner is universally valid with no problems attached. Something happened in the pastoral visit to the hospital because God willed it or wanted it a particular way. "I believe that God was involved. That's all the theology I need."

In contrast to such views, I believe that relating the events of our lives—particularly our practice of ministry—to Christian theology, although it is not a quick and simple process, can contribute both to a deeper understanding of Christian faith and a more effective ministry of the Church. Moreover, as the term "theological reflection" suggests, theological conceptualization does not grow immediately out of pastoral experience. At its best the process is slow. James and Evelyn Whitehead have taught us that there should be a "method in ministry" which is theological.[2] What I do in this book is similar in many ways to what the Whiteheads do in their work, but the essential elements in my method and some of the problems addressed are different.

This book is titled *From Ministry to Theology: Pastoral Action and Reflection* in order to suggest that there is a process involved in theological reflection. It moves *from* something *to* something—from the practice of ministry to the construction or reconstruction of Christian theology. The word *action* in the subtitle further reflects the book's focus on the process of theological reflection more than the results of it. The book begins with the assumption that ministers, lay or ordained, operate from some kind of theological understanding of what life is about, and that the practice of ministry can change that understanding in an important and creative way. It also assumes that Christian doctrine and belief are repeatedly constructed and reconstructed, not just by the professional theologians, but by ordinary believers who take their faith seriously enough to think about it. Just as a house, which a family lives in for a long time, needs regular maintenance and, sometimes, major renovation, so theology needs maintenance also. The wear and tear of life and ministry contribute significantly to that renovation in our beliefs and values.

The book is concerned with how acting on one's faith out of a commitment to ministry effects and contributes to the way that faith is conceptualized. Although it deals, at least to some degree, with thinking about many types of life events theologically, its focus is on "pastoral" events. The term *pastoral* however, is not a reference to the clergy alone. As I will argue later in the book, its primary meanings have to do with the responsibility to *care* and with the *accountability* for that care to a community of faith.

Action, Relationship, and Meaning

Many people have a limited ability to share what has happened to them in their lives. I have been in counseling settings with one person after another who could make general statements about the pain in his or her life, but who had great difficulty in describing the events related to that pain. In commenting on this phenomenon to my students I have described these persons as having flunked "Show and Tell." Somehow for them that basic, early-in-life experience of sharing what one has seen and done was devalued, and the amnesia about the events of life set in.

Over forty years ago a psychiatrist, Ernest Schactel, called attention to a similar problem: the loss of memory of the events that have shaped the course of our lives. He believed that we forget because we have not developed ways to describe and reflect on the events of our lives and share them with others. "Adult memory," said Schactel, "reflects life as a road with occasional signposts and milestones rather than as the landscape through which this road has led." The memories of the majority of people "come to resemble increasingly the stereotyped answers to a questionnaire, in which life consists of time and place of birth, religious denomination, residence, educational degrees, job, marriage, number and birthdates of children, income, sickness, and death."[3] If persons are genuinely to experience their human being, they need to reflect on, re-create, and share what has happened to them. Moreover, as we view that landscape from within a community committed to Christian ministry, some of the theological meanings lurking within the landscape may emerge.

Clinical Pastoral Education

During the past thirty years theological education has been influenced in its concern with relating theology to life and ministry by Clinical Pastoral Education (CPE). CPE, developed by Anton Boisen and others in the 1920s and 1930s, is concerned with relating religion to the deepest experiences of human life. Boisen's major concern was with the study of mentally ill, hospitalized persons whom he understood as involved in a profound human struggle—a struggle that had made them ill. There was, he insisted, theological meaning in what he himself and others experienced in their struggle to make sense out of what had happened to them, and he believed that theology students and ministers needed to experience and learn from it. In his attention to event and experience, Boisen followed in the footsteps of William James, who had insisted on the meaning and importance of even seemingly strange religious experiences. The validity of such experiences, according to James, can only be seen in the results they bring in the life of the person involved.

In his development of the clinical pastoral method Boisen followed James's view of experience and some of his methods in examining it. The events in the lives of persons were studied in case histories and pastoral conversations, later called *verbatims*. Although I have used case presentation as a major teaching method for many years, it has recently become important to me to use the phrase "pastoral event" rather than the more familiar term *case*. The term *case* is still determined in its meaning by the medical tradition. It may mean other things, but most commonly "the case" presents the medical history of a particular person who is illustrative of a general category of the diagnostic system. The phrase "pastoral event" emphasizes the uniqueness of the experiences of particular human beings rather than the medical tradition of the case conference. In *The Varieties of Religious Experience,* William James emphasized the importance of this by imagining the crab's outrage at being classified "without ado and apology as a crustacean, and thus dispose of it. 'I am no such thing,' it would say, 'I am MYSELF, MYSELF alone.'"[4] So it is with pastoral events.

In a wide variety of clinical settings students have been asked to recall in as much detail as possible what was said and done, for example, during a visit with a patient in a hospital room. At the beginning this is not easy to do, but with the suggestion that some notes on the visit be written as soon as possible after it, with practice, remembering events becomes easier. When the pastoral event is written in its final form, the student takes the notes that he or she has previously written and develops them into a narrative, which usually includes a dialogue between student and patient.

Obviously, what is written is not exactly what happened in the event. Seward Hiltner, one of those who carried Boisen's clinical method into the academic setting, often told his students to write in detail what had happened "by hook or crook, but not by sheer fabrication." Hiltner recognized that the use of imagination in writing the narrative is inevitable, but we may assume that the written event could be as useful in the student's learning ministry and theology as the event that actually happened.

Learning and growing in our faith from reflection on the significant experiences of our lives is something that should not be limited to students in a formal experience of CPE. As I suggested in my earlier comment about "Show and Tell," it is more essential than that. Sharing and learning from those events in our lives that seem to be "meaning-full" is important for our development as persons and as Christians. Sharing faith, formed by experience and belief, should occur informally in relationships with those who are most important to us. This reflection also can be structured programatically for what the Ephesian letter called "the equipment of the saints, for the work of ministry, for building up the body of Christ" (Eph. 4:12 RSV).

Interpretation and Imagination

In *Preface to Pastoral Theology* Seward Hiltner noted that, like any branch of theology, pastoral theology "applies some things learned elsewhere. But it is more than that." Hiltner sought "adequate critical study of events from some significant perspective." Such study, he believed, can make "creative contributions to theological understanding."[5] Don Browning, one of today's most frequently read pastoral theologians, has raised important questions about the validity of Hiltner's concern with the study of events as an adequate basis for pastoral theology. Browning has argued that under "the pressures of pluralism the very goals of our care often come under question." Our care, therefore, "needs to be guided by a more explicitly normative discipline—by a critical and practical religious ethics or moral theology."[6]

The popularity of Browning's work may indicate not only the importance of what he is saying but also some of the difficulty of knowing what to do theologically with clinical material or with what I have been calling pastoral events. Reflection on ethical principles should not, however, substitute for an attempt to relate our "meaning-full" experiences more directly to the theological understanding we have received and, hopefully, to the theology we ourselves are formulating.

Another factor, and point of resistance, surfaces when relating experience and theology. Many pastors are now trained by the hermeneutical emphasis in pastoral theology, which is explained in the writings of Gerkin, Winquist, and Capps.[7] Not only written documents but *human documents* can be interpreted, and appropriate hermeneutical principles, developed by biblical and systematic theologians, can be employed to aid in the interpretation. We have been fascinated with the hermeneutical process and its application to pastoral events since the late 1960s when we first read Robert Funk's *Language, Hermeneutic and Word of God*.[8] I have been troubled, however, almost as long as I have been fascinated, by the image of the "hermeneut" as primary for describing the minister. Karl Menninger suggests a problem with that image when applied to young analysts:

> Interpretation is a rather presumptuous term. . . . I dislike the word because it gives young analysts the wrong idea about their main function. They need to be reminded that they are not oracles, not wizards, not linguists, not detectives, not great wise men who, like Joseph and Daniel, "interpret" dreams—but quiet observers, listeners, and occasionally commentators.[9]

Although interpretation has a long and important history in understanding the dimensions of Christian ministry, I believe that the image can be problematic for ministers as well as psychoanalysts. There are equally important factors that must be taken into account in a theology that genuinely engages pastoral practice. In their book *Foundations for a Practical Theology of Ministry,* James Poling and Donald Miller have insisted that theology "must begin and end in the richness of historical-lived experience and interaction." We must, they continue, "find more adequate ways to speak about the richness of experience."[10] This book began with an event describing the pastoral practice of ministry, Doug's "historical-lived experience and interaction." It will end with another such event. Between that beginning and ending, it offers a way of speaking theologically "about the richness of experience" in pastoral practice.

Reflection on the richness of experience and thinking theologically will involve the use of the imagination. Although any theological model can be oversimplified, one of the most useful images for relating imagination, experience, and theology is found in Theodore Jennings's *Introduction to Theology.* Jennings suggests that human experience is a three-storied house. On the first floor is existence and reality. On the second, imagination and its product, the symbol. On the third floor, theological reflection. This image enables us to see that the events of our lives move upward to theological reflection and formulation by going through the "second floor," the imagination.[11]

In pastoral theology (defined here in a preliminary way as theology that focuses on data from the practice of ministry) there are three essential elements: action, relationship, and meaning. Imagination (a part of the larger concept of creativity) touches on and facilitates the working of each of these elements. Imagination stirs both individuals and faith communities toward action in ministry, relationship in community, and interpretation of meaning. In turn, each of these elements stirs imagination and creativity more than any one of those three elements toward the ultimate end of faith's practice: God. God's creativity stirs human creativity and imagination and empowers action in ministry, relationship in community, and interpretation of meaning.

One might visualize the relationship between the imagination and the three elements of pastoral theology with the diagram below:

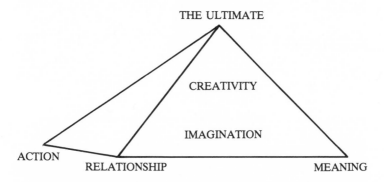

The imagination, from within the pyramid, is related to the three corners of the pyramid's base, action, relationship, and meaning. The apex is The Ultimate or, theologically speaking, God—the source of creativity and the goal of theological reflection. Each point of the pyramid's base requires relationship to each of the others, and each of these relationships touches on or goes through the substance of imagination. This book attempts to illustrate what this means in practice and to present a method for strengthening the relationship between theology and pastoral practice.

The first chapter, "Event and Imagination," deals with the rediscovery of the "meaning-full" events of life and how sharing them can activate the imagination and creativity. This chapter and those that follow it describe a method of working with groups of persons involved in a ministry of pastoral care and some of the things that have happened in those groups. Theoretically, the group method involves doing a type of existential phenomenology, and, therefore, some of the important features of that theory will be discussed. One of those concepts, "bracketing," is particularly important in understanding the slowness of the theological reflection process. Other theoretical material presented in the chapter includes some work on the relation of the imagination to empathy and the implications of research on the recall of pivotal events in the psychotherapeutic process.

Chapter 2, "Ministry and Community," further develops a theoretical basis for what takes place in the ministry groups. I use John Macmurray's theories of the self as agent and persons in relation to argue that a theology of pastoral practice, although it may grow out of the ministry events of particular individuals, is developed through relationship in community. Persons committed to and involved in ministry who meet together to share and learn from their ministry become, in my judgment, what theologian Edward Farley has called "ecclesial communities." In contrast to Farley and others, however, I believe that the development of ecclesial community supports rather than negates a professional model of ministry.

Important in this argument is the claim that the meaning of the term *pastoral* should be understood primarily in relation to the issue of accountability for ministry. A description of a group's experience of sharing and responding to "meaning-full" events continues in this chapter, but here the events are not so much individual experiences as those that describe the group members' relationship first to their kinship families of origin and then to their families of faith. The question addressed in the group is how *my* theology and identity is related to *our* theology in my family of faith.

Chapter 3, "Theology and Practice," details a pastoral theological method that focuses on a critical and corrective relationship between pastoral practice, the experience of community, and theological interpretation. The illustrative material from the groups involves the presentation of what I have called pastoral events and the groups' facilitating the dialogue of events with theology as it has been previously received and understood. The chapter attempts to demonstrate how members of a community of ministers in touch with their kinship families and faith families of origin can allow their pastoral events to speak theologically to the traditions of which they are a part.

A major assumption of the entire process is that an event experienced as "meaning-full" is already implicitly and imaginatively related to one's faith. Consultation within a community of faith can make that implicit connection explicit, and the event can speak to, enrich, modify, or change one's understanding of a particular theological idea that can, in turn, enrich one's action or practical skill in performing ministry. Pastoral practice and facilitating relationships each contribute significantly to the interpretative process. Pastoral practice can most effectively "speak" to theology when all three of these factors are significantly involved in the process.

Finally, there is an epilogue in which I look again at some of the questions raised by the book. There are two appendixes that give examples of handouts given to ministry group members at the first session of the group in order to tell them "what we are about." The material in Appendix 2 has been incorporated into the text of the book. The book ends as it began with the practice of ministry, with the presentation of a pastoral event, and with an imaginative theological reflection on it.

The whole book attempts to explore and support the thesis that pastoral practice and theology are related through the imagination and its empowerment of pastoral theology's three essential elements: action in ministry, relationship in community, and interpretation of meaning. In contrast to the trinity of I Corinthians 13:13, however, there is no "greatest of these," only the three together, each facilitating the development of the other.

CHAPTER ONE

Event and Imagination

It is not a good thing to work on a case scientifically while treatment is still proceeding—to piece together its structure, to try to foretell its further progress and to get a picture from time to time of the current state of affairs, as scientific interest would demand. Cases which are devoted from the first to scientific purposes and are treated accordingly suffer in their outcome; while the most successful cases are those in which one proceeds, as it were, without any purpose in view, allows oneself to be taken by surprise by any new turn in them, and always meets them with an open mind, free from any presuppositions. The correct behavior for an analyst lies in swinging over according to need from the one mental attitude to the other, in avoiding speculation or brooding over cases while they are in analysis, and in submitting the material obtained to a synthetic process of thought only after the analysis is concluded.[1]

Freud wrote several papers, relatively early in his career, cautioning practitioners who were minimally trained in psychoanalysis, but who could become so fascinated with its theory that they might apply it rather promiscuously in their practice. In this particular quotation I understand him to be saying, "Above all attend to the clinical material and do not mix it prematurely with psychoanalytic theory, or the patient will suffer." Interestingly, Carl Rogers said a very similar thing years later in his paper, "Persons or Science."[2]

The same principle applies in ministry as well as in the practice of psychotherapy. Students in clinical pastoral education have sought and found, with the aid of their peers and supervisors, dynamic insights about themselves as persons and ministers. They become aware of their unconscious motivation, the denied conflicts and needs underlying their behavior, and so on. They learn how to figure things out and become so fascinated in doing so that they stop listening. The process of learning to conceptualize gets in the way of their seeing, hearing, and imagining what is going on around them. Most ministers who have tried to preach and do a good deal of pastoral care and counseling in the same week will be aware of a similar temptation in the use of theological theory. It is very easy for pastors to find their counselees such good illustrations of what they are saying in their sermons that they stop hearing their counselees.

Adequate theological reflection on pastoral practice requires immersion in the clinical material of human experience, inhibition of hasty interpretation and conceptualization of it, and consultation about it with colleagues involved in a similar ministry. That is the major reason why reflection cannot be done quickly. That is why explicit theological interpretation does not come early in this book. But there are other reasons. One of them is our concern that the "meaning-full" events of life first be shared as they were remembered, not immediately translated into theological terms. Another is my belief that the cultivation of the imagination has not been given sufficient attention in pastoral theology.

Pastoral theology, as I understand it, is based on the belief that an event experienced as full of meaning is already implicitly and imaginatively related to our faith. Daniel Day Williams has stated that conviction in a more explicitly theological way. God, according to Williams, "is experienced as a power and process immanent in the world. . . . The dimension of transcendence is not excluded from this statement." Experience, as Williams defines it, is "the felt, bodily, psycho-social organic action of human beings in history."[3] Experience cannot be reduced to some part of it, such as perception, intuition, or feeling. There is a thickness and depth to it that is more than our attempts to describe and clarify it.

Show and Tell for Adults—Remembering, Imagining, and Sharing

The method described here has taken place with groups of theological students in year-long programs of clinical pastoral education. Parts of the method also have been used with lay ministry groups who have considerably less time to devote to the experience. The key factor in the success of the method is the commitment of the group members to deepening their capacity for effective ministry. The groups have been composed of six to ten persons, all involved in a ministry of pastoral care in a geriatric institution with four levels of care and in a large teaching hospital that cares primarily for the city's poor and victims of trauma and accidents.

For their work in pastoral theology, the groups meet once a week. After a brief introduction to the importance of memory and imagination in sharing events of life and ministry, each member is asked to write a story to be shared in the next meeting of the group. The story is to be limited to a page and a half and is to be about something that happens between the present and our next meeting. It is not to be a verbatim or conversation with a patient—the most common written material used in CPE programs—but a narrative that describes an experience that occurred in or out of the training institution.

Later in our series of meetings together there is a time for sharing and working with explicitly theological ideas about events similar to the story of the stillbirth which I presented in the introduction. Experience dictates, however, that the students should not examine "pastoral" events too quickly. We begin, therefore, with ordinary events of life, first from the present, then stories of past events, and then our imagined events of the future. We sometimes have written and shared types of stories that have been important in religion—myths and parables—or shared personal symbols or descriptions and diagrams of "holy" places. All of this has been our way of preparing for theological reflection on pastoral events.

We have learned over the years that even the most "meaning-full" pastoral events become conventionalized if those who share them have lost touch with their imagination and with the importance of relationships that help them more fully experience the events of their lives. It takes time to move step-by-step, but after the first anxiety of sharing an event in one's life with a group, it is a mysteriously satisfying experience. It seems to balance the anxiety and urgent demands for ministry in the clinical situation with a slow, reflective, community-building process that group members have reported to be "refreshing."

The following is one of the ways to structure the group sessions to begin the process of remembering, imagining, and sharing:

First session: Introduction to the value of capturing one's experiences and a method of sharing and responding to them;

Second session: Sharing and responding to events from the everyday experiences of group members;

Third session: Sharing and responding to events from the past, usually the description of an event from late childhood or early adolescence in order to get a pre-adult look at the world;

Fourth session: Sharing and responding to sacred places and things from the past (for example, a description of a home we lived in, a neighborhood, a special place in the home, or a symbolic object representative of an important part of our life);

Fifth session: Sharing and responding to imagined events from the future. Group members write about an event that takes place five years from the present.

In the first session the leader shares several stories from previous groups, for which the writers have given permission to use. Although we will not be able to ignore completely the writing skill of the sharer of the event, conveying what happens to us is not primarily a matter of knowing how to write English well. For example, a story was shared in a group many years ago by a middle-aged student from Thailand. Before reading the story the group members are asked to suppress their evaluations of what they hear and not to respond in terms of whether the story or even parts of it are well said or poorly written. They should simply allow themselves to experience what the story seems to stir in them and share that without criticism of what they heard in the story or felt in themselves.

This particular event was simply titled "An Experience During Past Week."

An afternoon during past week when I was through with my class schedule I walked along football field the back of seminary. After a long walk I went into the little woods with a feeling of like to get in there. I saw so many trees stood still with their falling leaves. I stood in the midst of the woods then made direction toward small hill in the woods. There was such a silence no sign of no one passing by. Also there was no cars running by as usual. I stood there on the small hill took deep breath. Down there was a little running water with the leaves floating along the current. Little wind blew the drying branches of the trees made little noise. This moment recalled during my days twenty years back when I served Thai government as forest ranger. I felt free from any disturbance. It called me of that day when I stood alone back of my campsite in the woods. When I walked further my step put on dry leaves sounded similar that day when I was in the forest in Thailand. This moment made me stood still like a moment of meditation. I felt like twenty years younger. It refreshed me a lot from this experience. I felt like to stand there for a long hour.

After reading that story the group was asked for their response, limiting them to five minutes or so. (We will spend a longer time responding to each of their own stories.) It is not a story that would be given a high grade in English 100, unless, perhaps, it was being taught to persons for whom English is a second or third language. I suspect, however, that even reading it in a book, you can feel some of the power of the experience.

The group members are encouraged not to respond too quickly, but to be in touch with the feelings and associations that are stirred up by what they have heard. I remind them again that they are not to be critical, either positively or negatively, and ask them what they felt as they heard the event reported and what they are feeling now. There is always a variety of responses. Perhaps the most common is similar to that of the writer: refreshment. Receiving an ordinary human experience from another without having to do something particular with it can be refreshingly different from the usual, somewhat competitive, settings for student oneupmanship. Competition cannot completely be removed (some persons write better than others), but it can be significantly reduced if the critical response is inhibited and group members respond with their feelings and associations. I have kept a copy of the Thai student's event for so long because it beautifully illustrates how much can be powerfully conveyed without sophisticated language skills.

Notice some other things about the shared event. It is very ordinary, but in its ordinariness it resonates with the experience of others. Almost everyone has had the experience of walking in the woods in the autumn, whether in Thailand, in Georgia, or somewhere else. Barriers of how each person experiences the world are broken down, and there is a sense of knowing the other person even though very little may, in fact, be known about him or her. There is also a breaking down of the particular time and place of an event. The writer was taken back twenty years to his distant homeland, and most of those who heard the event shared some of that transcendence of time and place with him.

Most important, there is no attempt to assign a particular meaning to the story. The group members had been asked to hold back on their impulses to give "the moral of the story." This is often most difficult for the writer. The question almost always present in both the writer and the group is, How can I justify sharing this experience if I don't say what it means or at least what it means to me? But this interpretation is exactly what the group leader should attempt to suppress. Later the group itself discovers, usually very quickly, the distraction of being told what something means or how they should react to it, and quite often they say something like, "Your story would have been better without the last two sentences. I didn't need your interpretation."

The structure for this type of group experience has developed over a number of years. As nearly as I can recall, the major early influences on the method were Ross Snyder and Eugene Gendlin. The latter was most influential in turning me to the theoretical roots of phenomenology in philosophy. I deal with the contribution of Gendlin's view of experiencing later in this chapter. Much of Snyder's contribution to me can be found only in my memories of personal encounters with him and with the vast piles of mimeographed papers from a seemingly infinite number of sources. Some of his method of "phenomenologizing" can be discerned in his book *Contemporary Celebration.*[4] Snyder was resistive to what he perceived to be a false type of community in the "encounter group" movement, and he sought an alternative type of group experience through "phenomenologiz-ing." Although what I am doing here is not the same as Snyder's phenomenologizing, I am indebted to him for stimulating me to develop the method in my own way and encouraging others to develop theirs.

Imagination and Narrative (Without Losing the Events)

The ministry groups follow a phenomenological method of capturing and sharing events in their lives. Here, and periodically throughout the book, my description of the group process is interrupted to present some of the theoretical material that supports this method of group leadership.

William James's classic book *Varieties of Religious Experience,* which has been important to the field of pastoral care since Anton Boisen, is a useful illustration of a phenomenological point of view and method.[5] In an attempt to get at the meaning and function of certain religious phenomena, James adopted a purely descriptive approach that avoided psychologizing or interpreting these phenomena in terms of something else. James's method "is to take a number of paradigm cases, to 'arrange them in their series,' and thus delineate some essential structures of experience under investigation."[6] His study was of religious experience as such, not of the origins of religious symbols of meanings but of the foundations of such meanings in consciousness itself. Although James was not a theologian, much of his work in psychology and philosophy can contribute to the practical theologian's ability to use his or her experience theologically. In *Principles of Psychology,* James points to the problem of living and thinking abstractly rather than concretely:

> *Every object we think of gets at last referred to one world or another.* . . . It settles into our belief as a common-sense object, a scientific object, an abstract object, a mythological object, an object of some one's mistaken conception, or a madman's object; and it reaches this state sometimes immediately, but often only after being hustled and bandied about amongst other objects until it finds some which will tolerate its presence and stand in relations to it which nothing contradicts.[7]

Similarly, when supervising students in their pastoral counseling, I listen to their counseling tapes, which repeatedly illustrate what James was writing about at the beginning of the twentieth century. A central feature of teaching and learning psychotherapy and counseling is helping students listen for the experiential, which is so often hidden underneath the categorical. "I have trouble with relationships," says the counselee, somehow believing that he is saying something that will reveal himself to the counselor. But in order to get closer to the person and have an experiential sense of what his life is about, the counselor must say something like, "Tell me about one of those relationships" or "What has happened that has caused you to say that?"

Like the present-day counselor or supervisor, William James sought to move closer *to the things themselves,* to the *primary phenomena* of consciousness, to establish contact again with the complex and concrete world of human experience. Although perception gives us our "primary reality," he argued, the perceptual world is not the whole of reality. It provides a "ground of possibilities, a virtual space which is indefinitely explorable." Thus in the most fundamental sense the world of perception is a world of imagination. To perceive the world humanly "is to perceive it as constituted of possibilities, absences, potentialities, of an indefinite number of other aspects," as well as future perceptions.[8] Ministers, lay or ordained, need help in discovering this process of imagination.

For James the structures of the mind can only be known through the description of this world as it is experienced and lived prior to reflection on the mental processes themselves. The object of thought, he insisted, "belongs neither to the physical world (the 'topic' or reference of thought) nor to the stream of experience but is rather the means by which we can objectify both consciousness, on the one hand, and things in the world, on the other."[9] He described "pure experience" as including "a *that* which is not yet any definite *what*."[10] These realities live not just in the knower but in the known; they live in the world of experience as well as the mind.[11]

In these brief statements James is taking on a number of prominent philosophical traditions, which insist that we are so separated from the world by the envelope of our consciousness that we can never know the meaning of the things we seem to experience. He countered that the object known is the object of the real world. Reason and thinking are not prior to experience as Kant would have it; they reflect rather than determine the structures of perceptual experience.[12]

The minister or practical theologian need not delve into the details of the philosophical debates of the late nineteenth century in order to see the value of distinguishing between "knowledge about" things and knowledge by "direct experience" of those things. In ministry to persons we are involved in that distinction every day. "Knowledge about" and "knowledge by acquaintance" are both involved in ministry, but the more important of these is direct perceptual knowledge by acquaintance. William James persuades us that conceptual knowledge was forever inadequate to the fullness of the reality to be known in perceptual experience or, as I am emphasizing here, in events.

A Psychological Focus on Events

Recent research on the psychotherapeutic process provides us with further reasons to recall important events. In contrast to the prevalent type of research that tends to look only at whole cases or the characteristics of whole interviews, some recent psychological research has examined clinically meaningful units or events within particular interviews.[13] Although this study of events is for a quite different purpose than the discussion here, some of what they have discovered is important in interpreting what has occurred in recalling and sharing events in ministry groups.

By beginning with an assumption that there are points in a psychotherapeutic interview that are particularly important, these researchers attempt to find a practical way to identify such events. Laura Rice and Eva Pila Saperia theorize that an event begins with "a client's statement of a problematic reaction point (PRP), so named because it is a point at which the client recognizes that his or her own reaction to a particular situation is problematic in some way."

In psychological language, a PRP contains three elements: (1) a particular stimulus situation; (2) a reaction that may involve feeling or behavior or both; and (3) an indication that the client finds his or her *own* reaction problematic in some way. "The client needs to re-experience and reprocess the episode in a way that leads to resolution."[14] Rice and Saperia point out that the therapist must try to evoke the client's own idiosyncratic experience in one particular situation and resist any temptation to identify patterns, compare with other situations, or otherwise move to a higher level of generalization or abstraction. In this method of systematic evocative unfolding the therapist is nondirective with respect to content but is highly directive with respect to process.[15]

The psychological researchers also found that one of the most common ways that clients move away from the significant events that they re-experienced in therapy was their tendency to react to their own reaction and focus on how irrational or undesirable it had been. They would expand on their childishness or irrationality or on the undesirable consequences, and the therapist would move away from the event with them, focusing on the secondary reaction. There is a similar tendency in the members of ministry groups that I describe, but the gradually evolving sense of community helps to overcome this.

The concerns of Rice and Sapiera are also similar to ours in their emphasis on "the client's maintaining a vivid and concrete re-experiencing of the stimulus situation. . . . The essential characteristics of the process seem to be re-experiencing and reprocessing, bringing to bear on the re-evoked experience an exploratory stance and a processing capacity that for various reasons were not available on the original occasion."[16] Most important, they say, is clients' discovering for themselves their own agency in determining the meaning of events and thus recognizing the possible new options available to them. This involves a vivid but focused re-experiencing of the event and the client's idiosyncratic construal of its meaning.

Again, the details and specific purposes of this research are not as important here as the phenomena noted, which also appear in significant relationships other than psychotherapy. For example, the tendency in both client and therapist to move quickly away from concrete events and toward generalizations even though the "saliency" of an event was consistently recognized by the client's feelings rather than by his or her cognitive judgment. The emphasis on re-experiencing and reprocessing events is also important. Rice and Sapiera note, as I have noted earlier, that some very important events in the lives of persons are not "claimed" when the event originally occurs. This is further emphasized by what they refer to as the clients' discovery of their own agency in determining meaning and the importance of their own "idiosyncratic construal." I would describe this latter point as the willingness of persons to use their imagination to re-experience and share the events of their lives.

Another contribution from this group of psychological researchers comes in an essay by Robert Elliott who (similar to the techniques used to help theological students construct verbatims) describes a specific method for remembering significant events in psychotherapy. The informant about the event is asked to describe in as much detail as possible what was going on before the event. Then, he or she is asked to explain in more detail what made the event significantly helpful or hindering, to describe the apparent intent of the speakers in the reported event, and to describe the immediate overt or covert impact of the event on the client. The client is the focus of the research even though the method for reporting an event is used for both clients and therapists. The informant is asked to describe what happened following the event, in particular, the further impact of the event on the client. Finally, he or she summarizes by describing the nature of the change involved in the event.[17] The value of Elliott's method for us is not so much in the detail of what he does, but in the importance given to persons' finding specific means of recovering and sharing what happens to them in their lives.

Empathy and the Imagination

"Meaning-full" events should not be lost, and a significant feature in this process of recovery is the development of the imagination. Psychoanalyst Alfred Margulies's book *The Empathic Imagination* is valuable to us in that it offers a discussion of the imagination in a relational context. The specific context, like that of Rice and Sapiera, is psychotherapy, but much of what he has said is quite applicable to clinical pastoral education and other groups involved in education for ministry. Margulies believes that phenomenology can serve as a needed complement to the psychoanalytic emphasis on the unconscious. He argues that Husserl's method of phenomenological reduction is comparable to Freud's method of free association. Both techniques, he says, prepare the subject to put aside the usual biases to observation and reflection.

> Whereas Freud's studies moved to the inner borders of the mind, where consciousness meets unconscious, Husserl moved to the outer edges, where consciousness merges with the realm of the senses. In probing the unconscious, Freud became aware of internal resistances, defense mechanisms that he broadly grouped as "repression." Similarly, in his exploration of consciousness, Husserl directed his rule of reduction to the biases in perception.[18]

Margulies describes the phenomenological method as clearing the perceptual field. The phenomenologists were trying for straight experience without interpretation, a descriptive psychology, not a "genetic" science. "Once we have learned how a thing is *supposed* to be, we experience it differently—and never again as directly. Maturity places an obscuring veil of understanding between us and the world." What needs to be done is "to deconstruct the body of one's elaborate contributions to perception."[19] These elaborate barriers and misunderstandings should also be removed in order to effectively reflect on pastoral practice.

"Therapeutic truth," Margulies continues, "is a dialectic, a creation of the relationship, a continuous coming into being of *possibilities* requiring further exploration." Furthermore, there is an element of surprise at the heart of both phenomenological reduction and free association. They were methods devised as first steps in the process of discovering unthought-of possibilities.

What the psychotherapist needs to be able to do, according to Margulies, is "to maintain an evenly hovering attention, to suspend the world, . . . the capacity to go against the grain of needing to know."[20] To "know fully *what* we are doing, to feel it, to experience it all through our being, is much more important than to know *why*."[21] The capacities of the psychotherapist, and I would add, the minister-theologian, are best described by either the German word *einfuhlung* or Gerard Manley Hopkins's term *inscape*. *Einfuhlung,* which is sometimes translated "empathy," means literally, "feeling into something." Similarly, Hopkins's "inscape," which seeks to capture the goal of the poet's imagination—illuminating the contemplated object from within, to chart its interior terrain—is a primary element in a pastor's learning from his or her experience in ministry.[22] Imaginatively to "feel into" the events of one's life, without analysis, is the goal for those who would move from ministry to theology.

Recapturing the Ordinary in Our History and Experience

If there is enough time, the group members are offered two opportunities to write about events that come from their present life situation. Sometimes, as with the Thai student whose event I presented earlier, that situation from present life resonates with past experience as well. We then move explicitly to writing about and sharing past events. There are many ways in which this might be done. Group members are generally asked to write about something that happened to them between the tenth and fifteenth years of their lives. These are often "The Wonder Years," when one lives on the borderline between adulthood and childhood and when the ambiguity of that borderline existence is indeed full of wonder about who "I" am and what life is about.

But the time in the past from which the story comes is not critical for the method. Here is an example from an earlier period in childhood.

"I don't think they grow around here," read a middle-aged minister to the members of his group,

At least I've never seen them, but for me there will never be any tree like a chinaberry tree. It's really not that impressive. As I remember it, it has dark green lacey leaves that grow in a kind of frond. And in the spring it has purple blossoms. It's not large like a live oak that's usually not far away.

But it has special meaning for me. When I was five my best friend was Joey Jones, who was a year and a half older, and it was over at his house where the chinaberry tree grew. We had washing machines back then, but for some folks the serious washing was done in a small house out back. The chinaberry tree grew right next to the corner of the wash house, and Joey had invented a game with it. You climbed up on the roof of the wash house by a ladder. Then standing on the roof you jumped off the edge to catch a large limb. The real part was called the "sass-shay." Holding a limb with both hands you could make yourself "boing" up and down like a kind of inverted pogo stick. When that was over you could let go, land on one of the benches that had been carefully placed there and declare your triumph. Joey could do it and so could Jim, another friend of his, but I couldn't.

I don't know why I couldn't but I'd get up on the roof, and it looked ten stories tall. And even with the calls, "Go on, sass-shay" or "Sissy, sissy, sissy," I couldn't jump. It seemed like months, although I suppose it was only days, that I hesitated, but the day came, hot, humid, bright. It was about ten in the morning. I climbed up, closed my eyes, jumped and felt the limb lowering me down, and then springing up and down. I had never known anything so wonderful. And Joey didn't wait for me to let go. He ran all the way around the corner to my house yelling, "He's doing it, Jack's sass-shaying."

At home they knew nothing of my struggle. And when I came home for lunch they were not impressed at all. "Don't you know that's dangerous? You could break your leg or something. Don't you ever do that again." But I did, again and again.

So on those rare occasions now when I see a chinaberry tree I really feel good. I wonder if they grow here.

If in this ordinary story we were concerned with the same theme as it appears in the work of a recognized artist, we might read and discuss Robert Frost's poem "Birches." The method of the ministry groups, however, is not only to experience together what the imagination can do with ordinary events in life, but to discover that ordinary "artists" can do at least some of the things that Frost did when responding to experience.

Thinking theologically about what happens to us requires the use of our imagination. And the imagination involved is not only that of the writer and reader but of those who respond to the narrative. By their responses, they add to the experience of the story by the group, and ultimately to its meaning. The group members demonstrate what we should already know—that we cannot effectively know, understand, or claim the events of our lives without sharing them and having others join in that sharing.

Openness to the Phenomena of Life

The work in ministry groups may be understood theoretically as a type of existential phenomenology that encourages openness to all phenomena as they are first perceived. In existential phenomenology the modifier, *existential* underscores both phenomenology's distrust of abstract categories and also the connection of the experiencing person to the event he or she is experiencing. The term *phenomenology* although it represents a concern to avoid the separation of subject and object, particularly emphasizes the disciplined nature of the method. It is not just expressing how I feel about something I experience. It involves an intentional, rational effort to allow phenomena to be experienced without my conventional ways of seeing and understanding getting in the way of that experience.

Paul Brockelman's helpful introduction to existential pheno-menology describes the method in this way: "Rather than *the* world which we assume we 'know' beforehand and which we use to *explain* our perceptual experience (sense impressions, etc.), it's actually the other way around: we can understand that 'ideal' world of objects only in so far as we take a close look at our ordinary, bodily, perceptual *experience.*"[23]

One of the most influential phenomenologists, Maurice Merleau-Ponty, has emphasized the importance of our pre-categorical perceptions in this way: "When I focus on my immediate experience," he says, "one of the first things I notice is that my experience to me as I live it through prior to reflection contains an implicit 'awareness.' The world is there before any possible analysis of mine."[24]

According to Brockelman, "the purpose of reflection is to make *explicit* what has been until this point merely *implicit* within our experience." Existential phenomenology is an attempt to evoke and verbally articulate the various dimensions and elements of our prethematic, ordinary, and lived experience or "existence." It is an attempt to get back to that whole interrelated set of preconceptual experiences and behaviors within the world of ordinary experience, in order to let it "show itself."[25]

I have made no explicit attempt in ministry groups to follow the steps in the phenomenological method that Brockelman and others describe, but what happens in the groups is in many ways quite similar. First there is the choice of a phenomenon or an event. Second, one must "bracket" all speculative and constructive views of the event so that there can be a disciplined "seeing." This is a particularly important point in the pastoral theological method I am presenting in this book. To experience the event, to encourage creativity, and to develop community in the groups, any immature or hasty categorization of events in theological terms is inhibited by the group leader. What is done may never be called "bracketing," and existential phenomenology may never be mentioned, but the group leader functions in the group to allow the bracketing to take place.

When instructing the group members on how to present their events and on how to respond to the events of others I ask them not to tell us what their events mean—to inhibit their tendency to interpret. This, I believe, is bracketing in practice. "One never will 'see' the phenomenon in question as it presents itself if one carries to it a priori views, assumptions, and assertions about it."[26] This applies to the ordinary events of life and to those that seem to demand theological interpretation.

Reflection on an event (in the group, writing about and presenting it) involves three things:

1. reliving the event or phenomenon in question through memory and imagination so that some primitive contact with the experience may be regained;

2. getting some distance from it so that it may be presented in words and not just felt;

3. putting into words an essential description of the phenomenon or event.

The method points to and evokes immediate experience so that those participating in it will be carried back to their own experience by providing verbal *"windows* through which they can become conscious of that of which they are *already* preconsciously (that is, experientially) aware."[27]

When a person writes about and shares an event in a ministry group "we make it change in our thought, trying to imagine it as effectively modified in all respects. That which remains invariable through those changes is the essence of the phenomenon in question."[28] Moreover, something quite similar seems to happen for the group members who experience the event in a different way by hearing it and sharing their responses. "Having encountered an event in immediate experience, we then attempt to put it into words, recognizing as we do that our words are fundamentally perspectival, intending experiential meanings which they never can fully or adequately contain."[29] This method is important, in my judgment, because it provides a structure for approaching the events of life more directly, and it enables others to share in them. Categorical and analytic knowledge is also important, but such knowledge should not blind us to things as they first appear.

Experiencing and the Creation of Meaning

A final concept that can expand and enrich the phenomenological method is the concept of experiencing. While attempting empirical research in philosophical phenomenology, Eugene

Gendlin became involved in research at the Counseling Center of the University of Chicago. Specifically, he gathered data on experiencing as those data were available in tape-recorded psychotherapeutic interviews. Experiencing, according to Gendlin, is a process to which we can always directly refer but cannot quickly or neatly conceptualize. A person's concrete experiencing "is not equal to concepts, conceptual patterns, definitions, or units of any kind. Patterns and units can be made from experiencing, but experiencing is never equal to what words we say, or to any 'what,' which one might define."[30]

Experiencing is primary over conception, but there is also a cognitive element in experiencing that may only implicitly be felt and not yet differentiated with words or symbols. Later, the person who felt that a particular segment of experience was meaningful may say that certain concepts do not accurately represent that feeling.

> The feeling, he will say, was such and so all along, but he didn't know it. He only felt it. He felt it in such a unique and specific way that he could gradually, by directly referring to it, arrive at concepts for it. That is to say, the feeling was implicitly meaningful. It had a meaning which was distinguishably different from other feelings and meanings, but its meaning was felt rather than known in explicit symbols.[31]

Although experiencing and conceptualizations are different, experiencing requires symbols both to point to it and to form and change it. Conceptualization is a capturing and completing process that can carry the process of experiencing further. When words and symbols fit there is a "felt shift," a release of tension and a feeling of satisfaction.[32] Experiencing is concretely felt inwardly and situationally felt outwardly. "There is no internal/external split; we feel internally our living in the external situation."[33]

Gendlin's insistence that experiencing is not subjective or individualistic but interactional or interpersonal is important to ministry groups because of its implication that capturing the events of our lives is not primarily an individualistic process but an interpersonal one. What a person feels at a given moment is always interactional. "Experiencing," he says, "is not 'subjective,' but interactional; not intro-psychic, but interactional. It is not inside but inside-outside."[34] "My sense of you, affects my experiencing as I speak, and your response partly determines my experiencing a moment later."[35] "It is not merely a matter of what *I think* you feel about me." I, as a person, am affected, even without stopping to notice, by every response of the other with whom I am communicating.

I have been presenting various dimensions of a descriptive, phenomenological approach to the events of life, in contrast to the psychodynamic one that has been so dominant in clinical pastoral education. One of my favorite illustrations of this contrast may be useful for those who are more concerned with attending to the phenomena or stories of life rather than to philosophical descriptions of why the stories work. John Schlein, one of the teacher/supervisors of the psychotherapy practicum in which I participated at The University of Chicago has used the following story to illustrate the perspective of phenomenological psychology:

The upper class parents of a small boy were worried. Their son was quiet, sensitive, lonely, nervous, afraid of, and highly excited by other children. He stammered in the presence of strangers, and was becoming more shy and withdrawn. The parents were embarrassed and did not want to expose their fears, but wanted some professional advice before the child entered school. The father solved their dilemma by calling a college friend whom he had not seen for years, and who had become in those years a well known clinical psychologist. For "old times" sake an invitation for a weekend in their suburban home was extended, and with some curiosity, accepted. After dinner, the mother "casually" mentioned their concern about the child; the father amplified this and suggested that after lunch the next day, the boy might be observed at play for a psychological appraisal. The visitor understood now the purpose of his visit, asked appropriate questions about history and behavior, and prepared to take up his assignment. He watched, unseen, from a balcony above the garden where the boy played by himself. The boy sat pensively in the sun, listening to neighboring children shout. He frowned, rolled over on his stomach, kicked the toes of his white shoes against the grass, sat up and looked at the stains. Then he saw an earthworm. He stretched it out on the flagstone, found a sharp edged stone, and began to saw the worm in half. At this point, impressions were forming in the psychologist's mind, and he made some tentative notes to the effect: "Seems isolated and angry, perhaps over-aggressive, or sadistic, should be watched carefully when playing with other children, not have knives or pets." Then he noticed that the boy was talking to himself. He leaned forward and strained to catch the words. The boy finished the separation of the worm. His frown disappeared, and he said, "There. Now you have a friend."[36]

The story needs no interpretation, only a reminder: "Listen for an event to speak before you categorize it."

Phenomenology as a Prolegomenon to Theology

Having discussed some of the value of a phenomenological approach in working with ministry groups, I turn now to the use of phenomenology in theology or, rather, as a prolegomenon to theology. Vanderbilt theologian Edward Farley uses phenomenology to identify the components and structure of the situation of faith. Comparable to the phenomenological psychologist's attempt to bracket out the categories of psychoanalysis or other theoretical formulations, the theologian using a phenomenological method brackets out "authorities" such as church tradition, Scripture confessions, and the "methodological commitments of the faith community." Attention is focused instead on "determinate imagery, social structure, and reality-apprehensions" of the community of faith.[37]

Farley's concern is similar to the intent of the ministry groups. We begin with ordinary life events rather than religious experiences in order to avoid the habitual ways of looking at reality and get beyond the usual ways of conceptualizing things. Farley seeks (as do the groups in the latter part of the method), to examine the situation of faith. The initial concern, however, is to avoid losing the situation or the event by applying too quickly the usual theological categories to interpret it. Farley examines the "matrix of the acts, language, and apprehensions of faith" or, more simply, what happens in the "ecclesial community." He probes the relationship between the community's intentions and what it actually does; for example, in the "inclination of a community of faith compassionately to relieve human misery," how the members of the community "intend each other as human beings," as they are "guided by Christological images."[38]

Farley uses the experience of the community of faith as the base line for his method (here I use terms other than his). Farley's focus on actual deeds (and not merely thoughts) is, in my judgment, supportive of a "clinical method" in which event and relationship are examined as data for theological reflection. For both of us a phenomenological method is "an instrument adaptable to a community of faith in many of its forms." It may, he says, "be a contemporary and phenomenological version of the nineteenth-century attempt to obtain the 'essence of Christianity.'"[39]

In describing his phenomenological method, Farley makes uses of Michael Polanyi's concept of tacit knowledge, which I use in the next chapter:

> No knowledge can be made *wholly explicit.* For one thing, the meaning of language, when in use, lies in its tacit components; for another, to use language involves actions of our body of which we have only a subsidiary awareness. Hence, tacit knowing is more fundamental than explicit knowledge: *we can know more than we can tell and we can tell nothing without relying on our awareness of things we may not be able to tell.*[40]

Farley's use of a phenomenological method is the starting place for theological work that seeks to examine the "everydayness" of faith. In the method I use for ministry groups, we begin by examining the everydayness of ordinary life events. Only after sharing and responding to events that are not explicitly religious, consciously and purposefully bracketing them out, do we begin to examine a person's and a community's faith world and the theology that grows out of it.

I suggest in a preliminary way that the early experiences presented in the ministry groups are illustrative of some of the ideas that Farley uses in the phenomenological method. In presenting material from one of the groups we observe how community is developed through sharing and responding to ordinary events. (In the next chapter I develop in more detail the view that the ministry groups I have worked with are in fact a type of ecclesial community.) The group transcript illustrates, at least partially, what Polanyi means by "tacit knowledge" and the "awareness of things we may not be able to tell." Moreover, in this simple description of what happened in one of the groups one can sense what Farley refers to as "the subterranean strata of imagery and intersubjectivity" and what Merleau-Ponty speaks of as the "ever slumbering part of ourselves which we feel to be anterior to our representations" and distinctive relationships that are ambiguous.

Developing Community Through Sharing Events

Another event, presented by a minister from the West Indies, may illustrate both the existential and relational dimension of the type of sharing that takes place in the ministry groups.

Saturday morning again. The sun was shining forcefully between the mountain and the hill. I was up early waiting for five friends. We had decided not to go to the mountain to collect dry wood, but instead to go to the hill and have more time to play cricket and if possible to go to the sea. We got underway. We were still excited about the cricket match the day before. It was my first captaincy, and we had won the match. We walked quickly along exchanging different foods with one another.

Before we climbed the hill, commonly known as the Gibraltar of the West Indies, we stopped and secured some pieces of sugar cane, making sure that the watchman did not see us as we ran away. As we ascended the hill we started to play the game of spotting the most monkeys as they swung and chatted and rushed along. We could not compete with the monkeys for the mangos, the cherries, and the pears.

We gathered the dry wood within the hour. Looking out to the sea we surveyed the different islands we hoped one day to visit. I wondered what a French island or a Dutch island was like. On the journey back home we tested our fitness and agility as we moved at a trotting pace. The tourists found us amusing and tried to take pictures. Once home, I would see my friends again, at cricket, or at the seaside or at church.

The following transcript is an abbreviated presentation of what happened in the group after the story was shared. The leader asked, What did you feel? What did you notice?

The first thing that struck me in the story was the contrast between the hill and the mountain.

I was struck by the sense of exploration and the sense of work and need to take the firewood home.

I liked the things we can't experience here—the monkeys going after the mangos, but also the commonality, the being with friends.

It reminded me of the three months I spent in Jamaica, the blue mountains, but maybe mostly the freedom of childhood on a Saturday morning.

It made me want to go to a place where there'd be monkeys around that I could count with my friends. But even more powerful than that was that he was one of the sights for the tourists.

It took me a few sentences to get over the difference in a hill and a mountain. I grew up in West Virginia where a hill was a mountain. I didn't know what you meant, but kind of went with it. Also I was struck by the kind of mood that you set, sort of dreamy and reflective. I was wondering, "Is this an adult writing or how the child felt then?"

I found myself focusing on the choice, Shall we do this or do that? The world's open to explore. There's this possibility and this possibility, and I remember how good that feels.

Another element in the method is the group's reflection about a series of shared events. Here are responses from the group when the leader asked for some comparison between experiencing the events from the present and those from the past.

I felt more identified with the past stories.

I kept thinking in trying to do this, "I don't remember anything from ten to fifteen," but every time somebody would read a story I would remember something like that which happened to me.

I enjoyed telling about the happiest time in my life. After that I left home, and it was never the same again.

For me, the time from ten to fifteen was the worst time I can remember. I'm glad not to be there.

It was hard for me to remember. I only have scenes, not stories.

You have scenes and parts of events, and you use your imagination to construct a story from the scenes you remember.

I'm not sure what we were doing, but it felt right.

Some Final Thoughts and Questions Raised by This Chapter

At the earliest stages of sharing ordinary events, group members often say or think, "I'm not sure what we were doing, but it felt right." If one looks prematurely for the end result—explicitly theological reflection on pastoral practice—the process is indeed a slow one. If one considers that mere recovering of "meaning-full" events in our lives and the necessary imagination and creativity involved in doing so may have value in itself in addition to the value of theological reflection, the time involved may not seem excessive. It may be reasonable to say, "It felt right."

In the early stages of the process, the brackets are put on in order that the richness of the events will not be obscured by hasty conceptualization into theological terms. In the context of relationships with other ministers committed to expressing a faith tradition, which we discuss in the following chapter, the brackets are gradually removed. Trust develops, and persons become more nearly able to speak honestly and personally of their faith. Pastoral experience is conceptualized and shared, consultation is given and received, and theological formulation takes place. The conceptualization is understood as strengthening the understanding of what ministry means and as undergirding a more nearly adequate and subsequent action in ministry. Persons go from community back into ministry armed with new insight and understanding but also ready again to put the brackets back on in the interest of being able to enter into the human situation of another person or persons.

As I have suggested earlier, the bracketing process is not limited to the way one does theological reflection in a community of faith. It is also involved in the way one does pastoral care and counseling. Helpful pastoral counseling does not involve an immediate use of theological words and ideas. Optimally, religious language is bracketed out for a while, as was the case with a young woman referred to me for counseling by her physician. After several months of working with this woman, during which her depression lifted, she exclaimed rather angrily, "Why didn't you tell me when I first came to see you that I was morally and spiritually bankrupt?" I replied, "When you first came to see me, we didn't know each other well enough to speak of things like that."[41] Pastoral care and counseling as well as theological reflection on ministry only slowly and hesitantly become theological—for fear of losing touch of the persons and events that call for theological conceptualization.

Although pastoral practice is barely touched on in this chapter, it is clearly presupposed. The persons involved in sharing events are persons with at least one common commitment—to be a minister and to carry out ministry. They vary significantly in the traditions they bring to the ministry groups, but they share in varying degrees of intensity a common commitment both to represent that tradition and to explore its meaning in their present locus of ministry.

Persons involved in ministry are not merely involved in experiences together to stimulate their memory and imagination, or to facilitate the communal aspects of their life together. They are searching for what Paul Pruyser has called "transformational knowledge." According to Pruyser the professional members of the disciplines of psychiatry, clinical psychology, and ministry, among others, gain a great deal of their basic knowledge not from impeccable theories but from practical engagements with persons they are attempting to help. "Transformational knowledge does not stem from pure, disinterested contemplation but is steeped in urgently needed meliorative—remedial, medicinal, salvational, rescuing—action."[42]

Although, to use Pruyser's words, "practical engagements with people" are not the agenda in the portion of the group life presented in this chapter, the common experience with them is the *raison d'etre* of the group's being together, hearing and responding to one another. The structure and leadership of the group facilitate openness and understanding, but the underlying dynamic for the ability of the group to work together and experience community with each other is the common experience in ministry.

One of the reasons for the poverty of theological reflections in CPE is that, as rich as clinical pastoral education can be in offering an encounter with those struggling persons whom Anton Boisen called "living human documents," CPE and the supervised ministry variations of it in seminary and in parishes become conventionalized. Ministry group members learn a lot. They discover new ways to talk about themselves, the patients, and their problems. At the same time many also learn not to "see" the events taking place around them. In the training center, most often a hospital, the richness of the setting can be lost in the learning of categories—the medical, psychological, or whatever the most common language of the institution is. Instead of learning to describe and share what is, they may too often simply learn categories that distance themselves from what happens to them. Moreover, there is a tendency for students in CPE to lose touch with what they are experiencing because they have become so enamored with analyzing the psychodynamics of a situation. This tendency may be expressed in a suspicion of everything that is obvious and in an assumption that a deeper meaning must be found in everything.

Thus the concern with the recovery of events has been, to some degree at least, balanced by the concern with the use of the imagination. Originally stirred by the dullness of theological reflection that was written at the end of verbatims of ministry events, my concern with the imagination is related both to overturning the assumption that all knowledge can be gained through analysis and also to encouraging the facilitation of relationships with patients and peers by imaginative sharing. Margulies' work *The Empathic Imagination* is an example of bringing together these two concerns. *Einfuhlung* is a capacity that can allow one imaginatively to "feel into" the life of one's parishioner or into one's own life experience. It is a capacity that certainly involves interpretive skills, but one that places limits on them as well.

In summary, the emphases of this chapter have been on event, imagination, and a phenomenological method that allows us to approach an event with minimal conceptual baggage into which the event must be squeezed. The existential and relational emphases of the various theorists I have discussed seem in different ways to demand that the knowledge we derive from experiences and events is far from a purely objective knowledge. It is not detached from the perceiver and knower, his or her involvement in the knowing process, or from the relationships in which the perceiver and knower are involved.

We anticipate at this point three objections to the unfolding method. First, isn't this process a long way (or, perhaps, the wrong way) to move from experience to theology? I am reminded of a story my teacher Seward Hiltner told one time at the beginning of a lecture. A young woman who was buying material for her wedding dress was asked how much of the particular fabric she wanted. When she told the clerk, "About thirty yards," the clerk was somewhat surprised and said, "Isn't that an awful lot of material." "I suppose it is," said the young woman, "but, you see, I'm a Unitarian; and for us, the search is more important than the find." In theology the search to conceptualize "meaning-full" experience is often more important than the find.

Second, are not all efforts to access event and experience actually interpretations of experience, and is not all that we are involved in discussing really a hermeneutical question? I believe that a consideration of transformational knowledge in chapter 2 will make it evident that there are serious limits to the all-encompassing nature of hermeneutics, even as there are limits on our access to the events of our lives.

Finally (perhaps the most important question about spending time reflecting theologically in ministry groups, at least for the church), what difference does theological reflection make, anyway? (Why should we bother about theology at all?) The most important thing is ministry. There are a number of reasons why I agree with that point of view. The evidence to the contrary will come, however, if this book is mildly convincing to the ministers, lay and clergy, who read it. For the persons involved in a CPE program and, I think, for most of us, theology is secondary to an emergency call to minister to a person or family in need. The fact that it is secondary, however, does not mean that it is not important.

CHAPTER TWO

Ministry and Community

We live in an environment which silences the sharing of the events of our lives. Our personal experiences are labeled as unimportant or, even worse, as a hindrance to our common growth. A genuine, non-critical mode is not easy at first in a ministry group. I listen to the stories of other group members wanting to decide whether they had acted appropriately. Yet quickly, apparently due to the non-critical atmosphere of the group, I am able to hold back this hyper-critical sense.

Eventually, at the most basic level, I begin to use non-critical but active listening in order to hear the events of my own life. I begin to do this almost without realizing I am doing it. I begin to see how critical I am of my own story and how this critical eye silences much of its meaning and renders it useless for my further growth as a person.

This striking reflection, written by a member of one of the ministry groups about what he had experienced, emphasizes the attentive, non-critical atmosphere in the group. He notes the difficulty of being non-critical himself. His first response is classification—deciding whether or not the person sharing an event or story had acted appropriately. He is surprised to find, however, that he is able to bracket this first critical response and to develop a mode of active listening to the other members. In doing so, he becomes aware of how the tendency to criticize and classify has inhibited the sharing of events and stories of his own life and the opportunity to learn from them.

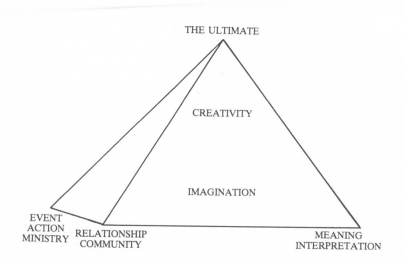

THE ULTIMATE

CREATIVITY

IMAGINATION

EVENT
ACTION
MINISTRY RELATIONSHIP
COMMUNITY

MEANING
INTERPRETATION

In the previous chapter, "Event and Imagination," I discussed the inside of the pyramid and its relationship to the left point of the pyramid's base, "event." This point may also be identified as action or agency and, when focused more specifically in a theological direction, "action in ministry," or "pastoral practice." Each of the base points of the pyramid is related to the other two. Each relationship is energized by creativity and imagination. This chapter deals with the relationship of the base point identified as "event, action, and ministry" to the base point of "relationship" or "community."

In addition to the image of the pyramid, the work of this chapter involves the image of brackets from phenomenology. The two functions of bracketing, noted in the previous chapter, prevented premature classification of an event as a particular type of thing, or hasty judgment about its value. Both of these functions of bracketing can be seen in the group member's reflections presented above: in his attempt to inhibit an evaluation response to what another group member had done and in what he calls "non-critical, active listening." The ministry groups develop a sense of community among the members, facilitated by an initial bracketing out of critical responses to what was shared. As relationships have developed in the groups, the brackets are gradually removed so that conceptualization, critique, and objectivization become appropriate responses as the groups move from reflection on pastoral event to theological reconstruction. The dynamic or moving force in this process is creativity and imagination. The structure for the process is the use of the brackets.

(Bracketed Out) Critique	(within the brackets) [*event, action, existential involvement*]	(Bracketed Out) Abstract conceptualization

Experiencing Community

The attempt to reduce the critical spirit of the group or, perhaps more accurately, the need to classify rather than to respond, is only a part of the process of moving from pastoral event to theology. But it is an important part. It allows the event to be re-experienced by the one to whom it happened and, to some extent at least, to be experienced by other group members. The development of this type of group response gives the event, and the narrative that contains it, an opportunity to stand on an equal footing and to speak to the more clearly conceptualized concepts of theology. In the reflections of all of the ministry groups I can remember, and from which I have collected data, the experience of community appears to be of primary importance. One person put it this way:

Slowly but surely, we began to grow as a community of faith. Faith in each other, which was fostered by our love of the Creator. It became clear very early that the group had a much stronger sense of community than of diversity. It was obvious that the group had differences, but a strange love relationship emerged that allowed the group to transcend those differences and focus on the common interest. As the group began to share issues in ministry, broad theological themes began to reveal themselves more clearly, and as the group experience continued, these themes became the focus of discussion.

The group was both the subject of observation and the

observing subject. It seemed to be involved in a *method* of theological reflection, which made the experience the focus of that reflection. Given a method and a relatively safe communal environment, the group found itself immersed in deep and profound theological reflection. The sharing of events opened the door for feelings and images in other group members, which were shared, and which in turn produced other feelings and images. The sharing served as a catalyst with seemingly endless potential. The non-threatening community allowed the method to stir creativity, which was a direct result of the methodology followed.

Another group member presented his reflections on the importance of community in this way:

> One of the most significant elements in the experience has to do with the importance of community. My story seemed to take on meaning and significance as it was placed in dialogue with other stories. Sharing stories in the group created a sort of "given" body of experience against which (here not meant in the negative sense of opposition) I could then notice the similarities and unique nuances of my experiences.
>
> There was true dialogue going, which produced new insights for me. The kind of non-critical association of stories before linking up with specific social or theological categories was helpful in that it allowed for more voices in the conversation at the same time.

Theoretical Perspectives on the Experience of Community

As in the previous chapter, I interrupt this presentation of the ministry groups' experiences to examine several theoretical concepts that I believe can assist in interpreting and presenting in a less personal way the groups' experiences. One resource for doing this is the work of anthropologist Victor Turner, who, in his studies of primitive communities, has revealed some of the characteristics of more sophisticated ones. Turner uses the term *communitas* to identify a rudimentarily structured and relatively undifferentiated community of equal individuals who submit together to the authority of a "ritual elder," a leader having been given authority by the larger community, tribe, or, in our case, religious group. *Communitas* is a modality of social relationship,[1] involving "immediate, concrete" experiencing as opposed to the abstract, norm-governed character of social structure. With its "unstructured character, *communitas* represents the quick of human interrelatedness. . . ."[2] *Communitas* has an existential quality involving the whole person in relation to other persons.

Within *communitas,* according to Turner, there exists *liminality. Liminality* describes, in part, the statusless existence of an in-between time. Those experiencing it in community are in process from something to something else. Turner uses the concept to describe the transition rituals that move an individual from adolescence to adulthood, but it may accurately be used more broadly to refer to any transition period when persons are moving from one condition, status, or understanding to another. *Liminality* is "bracketed" time when the usual ways of doing and thinking about things do not apply.

The ministry groups, in my judgment, clearly exhibit some of these characteristics. They have in one sense a structure that is rigidly imposed by the group leader—analogous in Turner's system to the ritual elder. That imposed structure, however, is a deconstruction of group members' status outside the group in favor of immediate, concrete experiencing within the group. In this sense what happens in the group is "unstructured," or at least it offers an opportunity for going beyond conventional social relationships and moving toward intimacy with one another.

Edward Farley's philosophical-theological perspective is also helpful in interpreting the experience of these groups. With dependence upon phenomenologist Merleau-Ponty, Farley describes ecclesial existence as the "ever slumbering part of ourselves which we feel to be anterior to our representations, to that individual haze through which we perceive the world. There are here blurred outlines, distinctive relationships which are in no way 'unconscious' and which, we are well aware, are ambiguous."[3] He uses the term "determinant intersubjectivity" to describe the "mutual intentions or ways of meaning through which participants in ecclesial reality are present to each other."[4]

Farley believes that determinant intersubjectivity can be understood by thinking of some of the characteristics of a marriage relationship. Marriage is determinant because it comprises not just the general conditions for relationship to anyone but the specific conditions of meanings of the other as an enduring mate and possible co-parent.[5] Marriage involves not just consciously chosen mutual affection or mutual commitment but a depth dimension of such a commitment, rarely formulated or even made the object of reflection.[6] If ecclesial existence is a basis for theology, according to Farley, then we should move beyond "the formal language of the community to the images beneath it, and work our way through its institutional layers to the underlying determinate intersubjectivity."[7]

Although they bring very different perspectives to bear on interpreting the experience and meaning of community, both Turner and Farley describe a way to understand ministry group members' experience. Although neither explicitly use the concept of bracketing in the material we have cited here, life within *communitas* and within *ecclesia* involves bracketing out the way things are usually done or thought about. Although the ministry groups focus on what is being experienced now, they are more like Turner's *communitas* than Farley's *ecclesia*. They also have a quality not unlike the special relationship that Farley describes as "determinant intersubjectivity." A special kind of relationship exists among the members, which produces confidentiality and commitment, and which is conducive to sharing "meaning-full" events.

The Self as Agent and Persons in Relation

John Macmurray's Gifford lectures have not, to my knowledge, had significant influence in the area of pastoral or practical theology until a recent book by Frank G. Kirkpatrick, *Community: A Trinity of Models*.[8] A central concern of my book is summed up in Macmurray's thesis for his Gifford lectures: "All meaningful knowledge is for the sake of action, and all meaningful action is for the sake of friendship."[9]

Macmurray's work attempted to overcome what he saw as

the egocentricity of modern philosophy, which takes the self as its starting point, "not God, or the world or the community," and views the self as purely individual "in isolation, an ego or 'I,' never a 'thou.' "[10] Macmurray insists that reflection must be done from the standpoint of relationality, which is possible only if the self is first a doer and secondarily a thinker. Persons, he argues, fulfill themselves in action that is intended to embrace others in mutuality and love. The thinker, in contrast to the actor, tends to isolate himself or herself in the thinking process, and as a result of this starting point tends to see theory and practice as separated from each other.[11]

For Macmurray, knowledge of the other is a presupposition, an alternative, non-demonstrable starting point.[12] Action, in contrast to thinking, "is a full concrete activity of the self in which all our capacities are employed."[13] The self is never exclusively engaged in theory apart from other dimensions of immediate experience. The unity of the person is affirmed by conceiving of the person as agent. It is through the practical encounter of action that the person knows that another exists. The other is discovered both as the resistance to and the support of action.[14]

In the second volume of the Gifford lectures, *Persons in Relation,* Macmurray becomes more explicitly psychological. He points to the mother-child relation as the most basic form of relationship. This bond enables the child to move from the biological to the personal.[15] The impulse toward communication is the sole adaptation to the world with which the child is born. There is also in the primary relationship an element of symbolic activity that has no organic or utilitarian purpose. The relationship is enjoyed for its own sake.[16] Prior to the development of conscious intentions the child has two orientations toward others, love and fear. Fear is the notion that the other will not respond and leads to inhibition of action and a continuing fear of making a mistake in relation to the other.[17] Because it is not always possible for the other to respond, relationship must include forbearance and forgiveness.

Love is fulfilled only when it is reciprocated, and it presupposes both individuality and mutuality. Macmurray describes the communal mode of relationship as an active connection of friendship and a thinking of oneself in relationship so that sacrifice for the other is not sacrifice of oneself. The unity of persons in community is not a fusion of self but a unity of persons where each remains a distinct individual, but each realizes himself or herself in and through the other.[18]

In this brief presentation of his views, I only touch on the richness of Macmurray's contribution toward developing a normative view of humanity and, for my purposes here, a method for pastoral theology. Although similar views of the relationality of human being appear in more recent literature, Macmurray's book is particularly helpful because it brings together action and relationship as inseparable dimensions of human being.

Our Communities of Origin and Our Present Community of Faith

A community described in action by ministry group members and in theory by the philosophers cannot be produced on demand. There are, however, structures and methods that seem to contribute to its development. The method of group leadership that seems to have contributed most is a non-critical response to events in life and ministry shared by the group members and initially facilitated by a rather rigid requirement for the type of response insisted on by the group leader. Also contributing is the structure or agenda for what is initially presented in each of the group meetings. The agenda used for the first five sessions of the groups' time together—focusing on sharing "meaning-full" personal events—was presented in the previous chapter. The agenda for the next three sessions, which are specifically focusing on communities of origin and of faith, is given below:

> **Sixth session:** Sharing and responding to myths and parables. Using the definitions that myth is a story that creates or forms a way of explaining the particular world we live in, and that parable is a story that destroys or undercuts one's way of looking at the world, the group members write and share myths and parables.

Seventh session: Sharing and responding to events that reveal how we are formed by and are differentiating ourselves from our families of origin.

Eighth session: Sharing and responding to how we are a part of a particular religious tradition but also differentiated from it—our theology and my theology.

Communities of Origin

The development of an experience of community is significantly related to our communities of origin. Most of the groups of ministers and theological students with whom I have worked have been committed to weekly meetings for an entire academic year—with only a few interruptions for holidays and required absences of the leader. Toward the end of the first semester, looking forward to the work of the second, the structure for the groups moves from a concern with individual events to the formative power of event-based stories on the life of a community. Although this particular assignment or structure for the group is not one that I always use—and not one on which I have collected much data—it has seemed useful in pointing out the influential power of events, not just for individuals but for families and larger communities.

The first of these sessions is labeled "Sharing and Responding to Myths and Parables." The group members have already shared with each other a number of different types of personal stories. Now they are asked for stories of a particular group, stories that have influenced the way the group thought and acted. John Dominic Crossan's definition and distinction between myth and parable can stimulate imagination. Myth for Crossan is a story that creates or forms a way of explaining the particular world of a small or large community of persons. Parable, in contrast, is a story that prophetically destroys or undercuts that world. Jesus' parables are the most familiar examples of common assumptions and expectations being undercut.

The field of family therapy contains much literature about family myths. These myths have both formative and conservative power in the family, with a lack of literal truth. In that literature the emphasis has been more on the lack of truth, their concealing function, and techniques of intervention have been designed to undercut the power of family myth. Actually, a simple telling of a mythic story to a group or person outside the family is usually enough to undercut its power. Although members of the ministry groups have had some difficulty in thinking of their family stories in mythic and parabolic terms, the following simple story shared by a ministry group member reveals a benign family myth, the parabolic undercutting of its literal truth, and how the myth functioned to order relationships within the family.

For as long as I can remember fruit cocktail has contained the basic ingredients of diced pears, peaches, and pineapple, plus two other special fruits: those beautiful red maraschino cherry halves and whole ground cherries. Ground cherries rose to special prominence in our family not because they were the only whole fruit in a dish of fruit cocktail and not because of their uniquely juicy flavor. Rather, ground cherries were special because they, along with the maraschinos, were awarded on a turn-about basis to each of the children. The scene was often repeated: Mom and Dad and the four of us seated around the table, supper nearing an end. "What's for dessert, Mom?" I ask. "Well, I think we'll have fruit cocktail," Mom says. Immediately we all four clamored, "I want a red one." "It's my turn for a red one!" We wait on the edge of our seats to see how many red maraschino cherry halves are in this can. There are never enough. "Two? But there are four of us!" "Well, here, son, I'll give you a bowl with three ground cherries to make up for the red ones." Second prize, to be sure, but ground cherries were still satisfying in their own right.

Several years ago, as we sat around the Thanksgiving table my wife and I commented on how good the fruit cocktail was and how much we had always enjoyed it. "I especially like the grapes," she said. Startled, I looked down at my bowl full of ground cherries. "My God," I gasped. "Those things are grapes!"

The story is mythic because it helps to bring order to the family and develop a meaningful ritual. The revelation that ground cherries are grapes is parabolic. It brings the mythic world of the family of childhood into relationship with the real world of the adult and reveals both the literal untruth of the family myth and its deeper community-forming truth.

If sharing cherries in a can of fruit cocktail seems too simple to be identified with myth, a story shared by an African-American minister presents mythic features that attempt to deal with a larger social problem and bring order to the family's life.

When I was eight or nine years old I remember my family's frequent trips to New York City where my grandparents lived. We would leave late at night, and my mother would fry chicken to include in our pack lunch. My parents sat in the front seat, and the back seat belonged to me. My pillow was propped in one corner, and my blankets and toys spilled off the seat onto the floor. I rode along, looking out the window at the lights, eating, and listening to my parents' conversation.

Some years later, I remember making that same trip to New York. We left early in the morning. My father, now a successful business man, could afford the luxury of scheduling our departure at his convenience, no longer tired from a full day's labor. My mother brought only a couple of pieces of fruit for a snack. No fried chicken aroma filled the car as we drove. When we got hungry, my father would ask us which restaurant we wanted to stop at. We arrived in New York safe and full, but the ride hadn't been the same. Was it traveling by day instead of by night, or was it the smell of chicken and the grease on my fingers?

Some time after that I shared with my mother my feelings of regret and loss when she stopped preparing chicken for our long trips. I remember her looking at me with astonishment. She had stopped frying the chicken because it was no longer necessary for us to carry our food. The restaurants that would not serve us when I was a child were now glad to have our business.

I have ridden the New Jersey Turnpike many times since my mother's revelation to me, and each time I seem to smell the aroma of fried chicken. Often the feeling is so overwhelming that I stop somewhere to get something to eat.

A second structure, which can be used as the agenda for one or more sessions, often happens naturally in academic year groups because the members often schedule visits to their families of origin at Thanksgiving and/or Christmas. The simple occurrence of the visit stirs up family relational events and stories. The assignment is to share an event illustrating how one was formed by and how one is trying to be different from the family of origin. The assignment is derived in some ways from Murray Bowen's concept of developmental tasks for the young or middle adult, or "differentiating the self from the family of origin," a concept that has been used widely in the literature of pastoral care as well as in family therapy. These stories sometimes have mythic and parabolic elements in them.

I prefer to use the phrase "recovering our tradition and recovering from it" as a way to emphasize both the positive and negative dimensions of relating to our communities of origin. A recent example of this recovery came in a ministry group from a young man who had largely cut himself off from his Italian Catholic family tradition and become a member of a conservative Presbyterian church. The story he shared in the group suggests how he has recovered from his tradition enough to recover it in his own way.

It was New Year's Eve day, and I was about to attempt to create one of my Mom's and Dad's fabulous Italian dishes. I went to the Farmers' Market and bought the necessary items: one and a half pounds of medium-sized shrimp, a half-dozen large clams, 16 cherry clams, 8 mussels, 4 crabs, two pounds of linguine (that's flat spaghetti), onions, garlic, parsley, olive oil, and a huge loaf of fresh-baked bread. On the way home from the market I suddenly realized that I was actually going to go through with it. I had to. I bought the stuff. I had to do something with it. When I got home I showed the family all the neat things I had bought. The crabs were still alive—the kids loved looking at them.

As I tried to remember exactly how Mom had done it the

last time she visited with us, I made a wise move and called her in New York. She wasn't in, but my Aunt Maria was. Well, being Mom's sister, she was no stranger to the kitchen either. So I told her of my grand plans. Amused by my endeavor and somewhat skeptical—I could tell by the caution in her voice—she proceeded to tell me exactly what to do with all that I had collected. Of course there were no precise measurements—cups of this, teaspoons of that. There never were. There were only the usual measuring devices that I had seen Mom and Dad use for years: handfuls of this, a little bit of that, a lot of garlic.

After I hung up the phone I had the funny feeling of knowing exactly what to do and at the same time not knowing exactly what to do. For about four hours I shelled and cleaned the shrimp; I cleaned the crabs; I scrubbed the cherry clams and mussels—all under the constant flow of icy cold water. I got the tomato sauce going and began to simmer the clams and mussels and crabs in the olive oil with onion, garlic, parsley, and some spices. It was at this point that the kitchen began to smell like, well, like home. I added all of the seafood to the sauce and let it simmer while the linguine boiled in the other pot. When I called the family to the table, each person had a plate of the linguine with red sauce on top. Shrimp were piled on top of linguine. Around the pasta I had arranged a few cherry clams and a few mussels. The crabs were placed in a separate plate. The large clams had been stuffed and baked on half shell. The feast was ready. It was really delicious, "just like Mom and Dad used to make," I thought, "just like Mom and Dad."

Again, little interpretation of the event is needed. What the group experienced was this man's recovery of his tradition and his discovery that he was capable of carrying it on in his own way.

Differentiating from Our Faith Families of Origin

Another structure can be used for becoming aware of the formative influence of our communities of origin. It builds on the concept of differentiating from one's family of origin. The specific assignment is to ask group members to write briefly on "How I Am Separating from My Faith Family of Origin" or "Our Theology (the theology of the faith family one comes from); My Theology (the theology that is most like where I am now in my life)." The assignment emphasizes two important elements in theological thought: the tradition received and the formative influence of particular communities on the way we understand theology. The following is an example:

The "our" of faith for me centered on my experience at the Presbyterian Church where I went through Sunday school, sang in the children's choir, was confirmed, was ordained a Deacon at age sixteen, and attended junior and senior high youth group. My parents gave a lot of their time to the church, teaching Sunday school, singing in the choir, serving on boards, and leading youth groups. Although I often hated attending church as a child, I grew up knowing it was very important to my family.

The first real sense of Christian community came during a youth retreat during my sophomore year of high school. The retreat focused not only on a personal faith but on a need to build community. Faith had always been for me more of an individual than communal endeavor. The sense of need for Christian community not only began to make intellectual sense to me, but I experienced it in the lives of my friends at church. During those years of adolescent searching, theology became most engaging to me and my friends, and we also began to do acts of service for others.

"My theology" was shaped by my family, my youth group experience, youth leaders, college days as a Bible major at a conservative Christian college, my field educational experiences, my seminary years, and the five years I have spent as a pastor. I have long thought that theology is, in a sense, anthropology. That is to say, understand the person, and you will understand his/her theology. I came to the point where my tight, legalistic theology no longer fit my anthropology. Looking back, that black and white theology was futile, senseless, and out of touch with where the people were. The idealism of my neatly wrapped theology didn't fare well in a chaotic, broken world.

Today my theology feels more real, more forgiving, less compulsive, less judgmental, less black and white. Years ago I felt very much that I had arrived and that I had the answers. Today I feel very much in process and that the journey has just begun. It feels okay if my theology changes tomorrow from what it was yesterday. That didn't used to be so.

As I continue on my journey of faith, I hope that my theology and my anthropology might be blended together more. I am not happy that I see life mostly through the monocular lens of individualism. I am working to see theology through the binoculars, where "my theology" is in one lens and "our theology" in the other.

I am not sure that this document on differentiating from one's faith family of origin is typical of those I have heard shared in the groups. This one does not go into the content of the theology received or presently held. It does not seem to represent a major "breaking away" from tradition. What it does do, as most of these reflections have done, is to affirm the fact of both continuities and discontinuities between what has been received and what the person now believes. This structure for theological reflection gives authority to recover from his or her tradition and suggests that what has been done before and what I am doing now are both important.

I have been examining different facets of community as a central element in moving from experience to theology. This has included the way community has been experienced in the ministry groups themselves. "Our heterogeneous community," wrote one group member,

was comprised of six persons who represented three distinct ethnic groups. There were two white males, two African-American males, an Asian male, and an Asian female. The ages of the group members varied from twenty-five to forty-five years of age. There were only two ecclesiastical traditions represented, Presbyterian and Methodist, but personal theological views were more diverse. Each member was a reflection of the member's own tradition's view, which forms and influences him or her, but each one's personal experience seemed even more influential.

"The thing that seemed to come through most clearly in our group," wrote another group member,

> was how tradition is both past and present. The group was a part of reshaping the tradition as it was evolving in the experience itself. It seems that tradition has both a sense of continuity and the potential for stifling growth. It would seem that tradition must have an evolutionary dimension that allows for reinterpretation, in light of contemporary times and experience. To not allow for reinterpretation would seemingly negate the viability of that tradition's relevance.

The Meaning of *Pastoral*

We now move to the second point on the base of the pyramid—action in ministry. The ministry groups are composed of persons who were actively involved in ministry, so this element is already influential in sharing events and developing community. Now, following Macmurray's image of the self as agent, we focus more specifically on the importance for theological reflection of the self as an agent in ministry. Macmurray argues that action, in contrast to thinking, is a full concrete activity of the self in which all of our capacities are employed. Thus persons fulfill themselves in action rather than in thinking. If this is the case, how is action specifically expressed in pastoral practice?

What is pastoral practice? Pastoral practice is not just the work of the clergy, although it is commonly understood that way. It can include the ministry of both laity and clergy. However, if we understand the term in an inclusive way, we must explore both the meaning of *pastoral* and the relationship of laity and clergy in being pastoral.

The term *pastoral* is considerably more than an adjective referring to the clergy. Although in the various Christian traditions there have been a number of meanings for the term, most of those meanings have involved either a pastoral "attitude" or pastoral "accountability." The pastoral attitude, perspective, or way of looking at things has most often been interpreted through the use of the biblical image of the shepherd. The shepherd cares for all but is particularly concerned for those who are lost or separated from the whole unit of care. *Pastoral,* understood as an attitude, reflects the joining of the meanings of the two words in the phrase *pastoral care.* Thus when the term *pastoral* is used in some contexts it inevitably means an attitude of care and concern.

In his essay on the theology of pastoral care Paul Tillich argues that because care is a universally human function, it cannot be monopolized or controlled by any profession, including the clergy. The difference between those who offer care as clergy and all other human beings is not that the clergy exercise this function and others do not; the difference is that the clergy along with other professionals consciously exercise care, reflect on it, and learn from it, whereas others express their care "indirectly, casually, and mostly unconsciously." Tillich differentiates between clergy and laity in the church at the point of intentionality. As professionals the clergy have a greater responsibility to learn from their experience and to embody or integrate what they have learned.[19]

By still following Tillich's basic idea, one may address the difference between clergy and laity in terms of "accountability." Clergy have a greater accountability for their ministry and a greater responsibility to deepen their ministry by reflecting on it and learning from it. Use of the term *greater* suggests a continuum relationship between laity and clergy on which clergy have a greater degree of involvement and a deeper understanding of the faith and practice of ministry. Laity have accountability for the same things, but to a lesser degree. The continuum image is a horizontal, not a vertical one; thus the clergy are not "above" the laity, nor do they perform their ministry apart from them. The fact that the clergy are "farther along" the continuum in the direction of professionalism has nothing to do with religiousness, depth of faith, or effective function. The image simply portrays the fact of greater involvement by clergy in study for and practice of their ministry.

The term *accountability* is helpful when defining pastoral

action, but to what or whom are we accountable? Brian Childs and I recently pointed to three types of accountability applicable to both laity and clergy, but applicable to a greater extent to the clergy:

> The minister is understood as accountable to ecclesiastical authority not primarily as a conduit for the church's pronouncements but as one who interprets how her or his ministry is an appropriate expression of God's calling to ministry. The minister is also accountable to his or her peers in ministry and sometimes to those specializing in a particular type of ministry for maintaining standards of good practice in the same way that other professionals are accountable to their peers. A third accountability of professionalism understood in its most positive sense is the accountability of the minister to himself or herself to advance in the profession—to become more competent and a better representation of what the profession . . . stands for.[20]

If both laity and clergy can and should be *pastoral,* even though the term is often used to designate only the clergy, the Ephesian letter's phrase "equipping the saints for the work of ministry" is an important statement about one of the primary functions of ministry. It suggests a view of the clergy as supervisors of ministry. As such, they are not "over" those being supervised. Supervision is a function of the clergy, not a superior status. The facilitation of ministry is itself an essential ministry. The fact that this functional superiority has often deteriorated into hierarchy is more an expression of the human condition of sin than a fault of the supervisory function itself.

Viewed positively, the fact of clergy-laity difference provides an important dynamic for the development of the church. The various movements in the church that have reacted against clergy control have been and continue to be important in the church's life. Within most mainline Protestant denominations we observe an effort to maintain some balance between clergy and lay leadership. The fact that this has, more often than not, simply resulted in covert rather than overt clergy domination does not mean that the principle is wrong. It means, among other things, that self-serving attitudes are as inescapable in the church as they are within other structures, such as business. The tension between clergy and laity is an ongoing reality that expresses the fact that each tends to get out of touch with the other and both need continually to work with the tension caused by that separation. Clergy expertise, like the expertise of any other profession, needs to be challenged by the laity in order to prevent its being used to dominate rather than to serve.

What Practice Is Not

In exploring the meaning of "pastoral practice" I have discussed the meaning of *pastoral*. Perhaps the most effective work in describing what *practice* is not has been done by Edward Farley. Through his critical concern with the so-called "clerical paradigm" Farley's work can help us understand more clearly what practice is not. The clerical paradigm, as he conceptualizes it, is

> the attempt to make discrete, public, and congregational tasks of the ministry the rationale and unity of theological studies. More specifically, this means that the areas and disciplines of theological study either directly deal with those tasks or find their justification in dealing with those tasks.[21]

Farley sees the emphasis in theological schools on functional tasks of ministry as leading to the uncritical importation of theories and methods from non-theological fields, such as psychology, sociology, and management science. This results in "a non-theological approach to church leadership because it permits a set of negotiations or unstated expectations between minister and congregation to determine the leader's nature."[22] His positive proposal to correct the deficiencies of the clerical paradigm involves theological education that develops a personal and existential wisdom which is not tied to any specific course of studies such as clergy education.[23] Farley calls this "wisdom" *theologia,* and argues that it provides theological rather than a non-theological criterion for church leadership.

In his critique of the clerical paradigm Farley has effectively described what pastoral practice is not. It is not something done with technical efficiency according to a manual for counseling skills, organizational development, or public speaking. Those manuals certainly do exist, and viewed and interpreted from the pastoral perspective described in the previous section they may be useful. More important, however, pastoral practice and professional practice at their best are not separable from the persons practicing. Farley has clarified what practice is not by too simply identifying clergy education and a professional model of ministry with the instrumental expertise or "doing" aspects of the clergy role apart from the necessary "being" aspects of that role and function. The *practice* in "pastoral practice" is not "technical rationality," the term used negatively by Donald Schoen in his studies of how professionals practice and teach their professions.

"The model of technical rationality," says Jackson W. Carroll, a major proponent of the professional model of ministry, "simply does not fit the actual practice of reflective practitioners." Perhaps the key characteristic of genuinely professional persons is that they

> recognize the plurality of ends which may be sought in a particular situation, making it necessary for them to choose among the ends in light of their values, their commitments to particular overarching theories and the strategies implicit in them, and their understanding of their own role in the situation. There is also the necessity for openness to "talk-back" from the situation, making reflective practice much more a transactional conversation with the situation than an objective, detached relationship implied by technical rationality.[24]

Professional practice is not the application of technical rationality apart from the person and the values and commitments of the person doing the practice. A similar point is made by ethicist and long-time authority on ministry theory, James Gustafson, who has emphasized the importance of bringing together the meaning of profession and calling:

> A "calling" without professionalization is bumbling, ineffective, and even dangerous. A profession without a calling, however, has no taps of moral and human rootage to keep motivation alive, to keep human sensitivities and sensibilities alert, and to nourish a

proper sense of self-fulfillment. Nor does a professional without a calling easily envision the larger ends and purposes of human good that our individual efforts can serve.[25]

Gustafson's view that professional practice is the expression of a "calling" underscores what has been said here about what the practice of ministry is not. It is not the employment of communication or management skills apart from the involvement of the person using such skills or apart from the community of faith authorizing them. The practice of Christian ministry is not developed apart from the "wisdom" that Farley calls *theologia,* but in dialogue with it. It is not the application of what Schoen and Carroll have called technical rationality.

What Practice Is

Practice, according to Macmurray, is the "full concrete activity of the self in which all of our capacities are involved." Without room to describe "all" of the capacities involved in practice that is pastoral, I will examine three of the most important: the capacity to facilitate change; the capacity to risk one's self; and the capacity to offer more than words. Because persons are in relation to one another, these are not capacities which are possessed apart from relationship but which are actualized in relation to other persons.

Change. The first of these three capacities, the capacity to facilitate change, is present in the concept of transformational knowledge. Our concern to help or change persons affects the type of knowledge that one can obtain.

> It has always been the business of the religio-theological enterprise to *transform* people, not just to *know* what people are. The same holds true for psychiatry and a good portion of psychology and sociology, whose practitioners are always under pressure from urgent needs to make meliorative interventions—even when basic knowledge is shaky or lacking. The professional members of these disciplines . . . derive a great deal of the allegedly "basic science" knowledge not from impeccable theories but from practical engagements in which they often have to make innovative decisions, not infrequently by intuition.[26]

Transformational knowledge involves intuition, wisdom, and mystery in contrast to technical control. Applied to the practice of ministry, these capacities are similar to what Farley appears to mean by *theologia*. Transformational knowledge is a "peculiar amalgam, different from the methodical knowledge sought by the humanities in their academic and scholarly pursuits. Members of the transformational disciplines are always faced with the 'messy' aspects of human life."[27]

Pastoral practice involves the capacity to encourage change, and it is subject to the critique: Did this ministry appear to facilitate change? This is not quite the same as asking, Did it work? Neither can one fully escape pragmatic criteria for evaluating ministry, because the Gospel writers describe Jesus applying such criteria to his own ministry: "The blind receive their sight and the lame walk, lepers are cleansed and the deaf hear, and the dead are raised up, and the poor have good news preached to them" (Matt. 11:5, RSV). Life-changing events happened to persons.

A useful counterpoint to the "transformational" understanding of pastoral practice has come from Stanley Hauerwas and William H. Willimon who have described the minister's need to help persons as sentimentality and, ultimately, unbelief. They point realistically to the importance and difficulty of pastors in setting boundaries on what they can do to help people. "With no clear job description, no clear sense of purpose other than the meeting of people's needs, there is no possible way for the pastor to limit what people ask of the pastor." The church was not intended to be an inclusive or accommodating community but an exclusive, story-formed colony. In our worship we retell and are held accountable to the story about what God is doing with us through Christ. Thus all ministry can be evaluated by an essentially liturgical criterion: How well does this act of ministry enable people to be with God?[28]

The critique by Hauerwas and Willimon looks familiar because clergy are eager to have their guilt stirred and served to them in various forms. This approach calls for a return to a genuinely religious ministry in contrast to a professional one. The ministry, understood as one of the other professions, is viewed by Hauerwas and Willimon like idolatry in the Old

Testament, a kind of yearning for the foreign gods. They assume, incorrectly I think, that professionalism and religion necessarily conflict destructively with each other. The tension is there, I agree, but it is a potentially healthy one. Professional knowledge can facilitate the practice of true religion both in the counseling office and in the congregation.

The Hauerwas/Willimon critique is on target, however, when their point of view questions our tendency to embrace a professional model that identifies health with salvation. I am not sure if this confusion has ever been declared a heresy. But this over-identification is as old as the attempt to purchase the apostles' gift of healing, recorded in the book of Acts. The real danger of professionalism appears in the over-valuing of specialization, which leads to identifying a part or a sign of the message of salvation with the whole. Because professional expertise is a good thing that can accomplish much which appears to be of value and is in some way related to the central message of the faith, it is easy to lose touch with the larger message. Hauerwas and Willimon remind us of our primary purpose. But pastoral practice necessarily has within it a transformative capacity.

Risk. The second capacity, the capacity to risk one's self in the practice, is implied in what has been said about transformational knowledge and the risk involved in encouraging change in another person. One might speak of this as the existential dimension of ministry. Or, as I have said elsewhere, ministry involves the "quest for unity between one's action and being," what one is and what one does.[29]

By necessity the pastor must risk the self in the practice of ministry. This risk is underscored in John D. Caputo's interpretation of Kierkegaard's concept of repetition.[30] The conviction of Johannes Climacus, the central figure in Kierkegaard's *Repetition,* that he must make life difficult through repetition, referred not to a *re*production of past events but to a creative *pro*duction of events and action. Repetition for Kierkegaard involves knowledge that pushes ahead as it repeats, that makes a life for itself in the midst of the difficulties of the flux. In repetition, who one is and what one does are significantly related to each other.

Caputo contends that philosophical hermeneutics (which is presently influencing pastoral theology) is a reactionary gesture, an attempt to avoid action by engaging in metaphysical speculation. He describes Hans-Georg Gadamer's doctrine, "fusion of horizons," as "the wedding of the epochs, the perpetuation of the life of the tradition."[31] He turns instead to Søren Kierkegaard, who believed that philosophy, particularly metaphysics, inevitably undermines action. Kierkegaard's concept of repetition, in contrast, is the power of the individual to forge a personality out of the chaos of events, in the midst of the flux, the power to create an identity in the face of the incessant dispersal of the self. Self is not a substance or permanent presence but a task to be achieved. The self is defined as choice—something to be won. Kierkegaard's concern is to move away from abstraction and restore the sphere of actuality and involve the person in action. This emphasis on the involvement of the self and the necessity of risk is also an essential dimension of pastoral practice. However "professional" the lay or clergy minister becomes, the risk of foolishness and failure is an ever present part of what ministry means.

Relationship Beyond Words. The third capacity involved in pastoral practice is the capacity to offer in relationship a benefit which goes beyond words. Ministry involves the presence of God as well as human involvement, but this is not what I am speaking of here. Rodney J. Hunter describes this capacity, in part, as "practical knowledge."[32] The philosopher Michael Polanyi leads Hunter to assert that practical knowledge of how to do something is literally beyond words. Elements of this knowledge can be given in principles and illustrations, but these fall short of enabling a person to perform a skill. Exactly how to perform the skill remains inarticulable. Scientific knowledge, he says, "entails an essential element of subjectivity because it is based upon and derived from the inarticulate skills of the scientific community— skills of observation, performance, judgment."[33]

Polanyi's concept of *tacit knowledge* enables Hunter to argue that the tacit knowledge involved in religious *skill*—knowing how to perform, perceive, and comprehend religious meanings—inevitably constitutes the context of theological knowledge. This, Hunter says, should be acknowledged and allowed to shape theology's goal, method, and self-understanding. Hunter indirectly acknowledges indebtedness to what was presented above as the focus of the professional model, namely that practical knowledge always involves some relationship to the whole person or the self. The professional, the employer of practical knowledge, trusts himself or herself and develops his or her own way of doing things. Practical knowledge involves a sense of context; wholeness that exceeds what can be known, done, and said; and a sense of oneself as a participant in the larger whole. Even more broadly conceived than that, Hunter believes that practical knowledge involves a sense of being in tune with or participating rhythmically in the world, accepting and being able to deal realistically with the way things are. (Practical knowledge, as Hunter describes it, would appear to be an important part of the wisdom, which Farley names *theologia*.)

Clearly related to practical knowledge is a capacity to participate in and to use ritual, formal or informal, religious and not specifically religious. Pastoral practice that is too dependent on words or ideas is limited when the situation for ministry calls for more than words or is in some way illustrative of the biblical symbol of "the confusion of tongues." While not directly addressing the issue of pastoral practice but indirectly contributing quite significantly to it, Ronald Grimes argues for the importance of ritual knowledge as a balance to and a critique of narrative knowledge in theology. He makes use of an article by ethicist Paul Ramsey to argue against the dominance of narrative on theology: "As we enact ritually, so we narrate theologically and act ethically."[34] Ramsey says that the order ought to be reversible and that all three activities should be on a par with one another. "There is no good reason for assuming that narrative is more foundational, more human, or more conducive to selfhood [than ethics and ritual]."[35]

Grimes argues that "performance-based metaphors (the word as stage, interaction as ritual, social conflict as drama) have wider applicability [than narrative] . . . because they do not imply that storytelling, or worse, literacy, is a condition of human selfhood."[36] "We are," he says, "afraid that if enactment were to take its place alongside narration, we would have to perform, that is, do good works or do something other than write and speak in order to be religious." Moreover, fascination with narrative can be a substitute for action. This is a point that was particularly emphasized by Kierkegaard, who

> embodied and understood, but could not therefore escape, the paralysis of hyper-reflection. Whereas he knew that at some point one had to escape the hermeneutical circling with a leap, post-modern theology has become increasingly snarled in it. . . . Theology ought to have many objects, not just one, and certainly not just language, itself.[37]

These dimensions of practice (change, risk, relationship beyond words) are recalled in a pastoral event that illustrates the possibilities which may be present in pastoral relationships. These events do not make much sense in terms of their verbal content but are, in spite of that, "meaning-full" events.[38] One can clearly see the importance of ritual and the limits of language in this experience of a young minister with an elderly, disoriented patient.

Patient: You may not be able to find me. They change my street so often. The street has had a whole bunch of names. 430-B. 430-B (her room number) is my street. I think that's right.

Chaplain: That's dead right.

Patient: Mary Jane Douglas, 430 . . .

Chaplain: B.

Patient: What's your name?

Chaplain: (I tell her, and she writes my name, address, phone number on the napkin she's been wiping her mouth with and asks me to sign it. I do and I'm hers.)

Patient: I don't know who we are or why we're here.

Chaplain: I'm Ron Gordon. You're Mary Jane Douglas.

Patient: Yes. That's who we are.

Chaplain: Why are we here, Mary Jane?

Patient: Because we like each other. You and me, we have fun. That's why.

Chaplain: (I'm a bit stunned and feel as if I'm walking on clouds.) You're amazing—absolutely amazing. (We laugh.)

Patient: Why?

Chaplain: You know more about why we're here than I do.

Patient: Let's get some ice cream. It would taste good.

Chaplain: And I'll buy it for us. (I have some sent up. We go into another room to eat it.)

Patient: Like it?

Chaplain: You don't think I gobble like this for nothing, do you? (She grins. We eat in silence.)

Patient: This makes me sleepy. (She lays her head down. A nurse walks by.)

Nurse: Miss Douglas, don't go to sleep on the chaplain.

Patient: (She snaps up alertly.) Don't get excited, nurse. I'm sleeping on the table, not on the chaplain. (Laughter from everyone.)

Chaplain: (kidding) Miss Douglas, I'm getting out of here before you do go to sleep and someone starts a scandal about both of us.

Patient: You're ice cream.

Chaplain: Why do you say that?

Patient: You taste good.

Chaplain: You do too, Miss Douglas. You really do.

The dimensions of practice, the capacities that I have been discussing are all involved in this pastoral event: the practical knowledge of how to do things, which is far more than learning "helpful" verbal interactions; the transformational knowledge or experience of change, which can result from even "impossible" situations; the ritual knowledge, which, like a sacrament, is far more than the words that explain its meaning; and the existential knowledge, which demands the involvement of the whole person, not just what he or she can do or think. I have only suggested the importance of these capacities or dimensions of practice for ministry. Each capacity is involved in the kind of understanding of human being suggested by Macmurray's image of the self as relational through full concrete activity, in which all of our capacities are involved.

Summary and Unanswered Questions

Pastoral theology, understood as theology that focuses on data from the practice of ministry, contains three essential elements: action, relationship, and meaning. This chapter contained two of those elements: action and relationship, more specifically, action in ministry and relationship in a community of persons committed to and involved in ministry. The discussion focused on clarifying the meaning of those two base points of the pyramid and suggested some of the ways that they are related. The other image presented in the book, the bracket, enables us to exclude premature formulations of meaning and concentrate instead on the formation of community.

To argue theoretically for the importance of these base points and their relationship to each other, I have used John Macmurray's view of the human self as formed by action for the sake of relationship. Macmurray presented an alternative to Descartes' view of a human being who exists because he or she thinks. Macmurray's person exists because she or he acts and is related to others. Pastoral theology, as I understand it, is based on this understanding of human being. In addition to Macmurray, I made use of Victor Turner's view of *communitas* and Edward Farley's concept of ecclesial community to interpret and conceptualize more objectively the experiences reported by members of the ministry groups.

The chapter then moved to an argument about the meaning of *pastoral* to make the point that action in ministry is a particular type of human action. *Pastoral* is best understood not as an adjectival synonym for clergy, but as descriptive of persons, lay or ordained, with a commitment to and an accountability for ministry. The image of a continuum is used to distinguish between clergy and laity, suggesting that the functional difference between them could best be described in terms of degree of accountability to the larger community authorizing ministry. This discussion is also intended to argue that the type of reflective movement from ministry to theology described in the book is not relevant for the clergy alone, but for all persons committed to ministry.

Action in ministry growing out of relationship to a faith community is then described not in terms of its authorization, as in the discussion of *pastoral*, but in terms of what it is not and what it is. Action in ministry has too often been identified as technical skills in such things as speaking, counseling, management, and so on—doing things to or with people apart from personal risk and involvement. Action in ministry, in fact, involves the more profound meanings of the concept of professional. I identified three of these: the capacity for encouraging change, for risking oneself in decisions about what needs to be done, and for making use of practical and ritual knowledge that goes beyond words.

Interwoven with the theoretical material were reflections on the experience of community in the ministry groups, family myths and parabolic discoveries about the truth and untruth of the myths, stories of identity with and separation from the families of origin. The final illustration demonstrated how action in ministry is sometimes beyond words. One can see in the illustrative material the formative power of myth and the prophetic revelation of parable in defining the nature of family communities of origin. I believe that the same process occurs in our faith communities, but I do not yet have material to demonstrate that belief. An example of a faith community myth for a United Methodist like myself might be the system of itineracy as a formative concept for defining ministry. The myth can be undermined parabolically with particular examples of its failure to work in today's world.[39] I believe that there are comparable examples in every faith community.

There is in the chapter some discrepancy between the theoretical and illustrative sections. There is considerably more discussion of action in ministry than in illustration of that action.

There are two reasons for this. First, all of the material in chapter 3 involves pastoral events and is illustrative of the sections on pastoral practice. The theoretical discussion in this chapter prepares the way for the interpretation of ministry events in the chapter that follows. Second, this deferral of ministry events to the next chapter is a further illustration of the method of bracketing, of discussing action and relationship primarily in non-theological terms before taking off the brackets and discussing them theologically.

The primary questions left for further discussion have to do with the relation of the inside of the pyramid to the base points of action and relationship. How does imagination stir both individuals and faith communities toward action in ministry and relationship in community? How, in turn, do base points of the pyramid stir imagination and creativity beyond any one of those three elements toward the end of faith's practice and of theology, the ultimate or God? These questions will be partially answered in chapter 3, "Action and Interpretation," and further addressed in the epilogue that follows it.

CHAPTER THREE

Action and Interpretation

My experience in the group confirmed for me that there is a link between experience and theology, but I do not yet know exactly what that link is. I think that it has something to do with the concept and experience of community. Perhaps I have focused on community as central due to the importance that the Reformed tradition has consistently placed on community as the crucial vehicle for a proper understanding of God's will. Yet, the experience of the group for me suggested that the move from my personal experience to some theological articulation came most profoundly when my experience was placed in dialogue with the stories and associations of the group. In this way my own vested interests were held at bay and my own blindness to other parts of my experience were exposed.

The Slowness of Getting There

This chapter describes some of the process and some of the issues involved in moving from action to interpretation, from pastoral event to theology. I focus on the theological method of *sharing* pastoral events in a community of ministers, *responding* to the events as persons, ministers, and members of a faith community, and *consulting* with each other as to how the relationship between the event and the faith one has received may be further explored and enriched.

Why has it taken so long to arrive at this point? Much of what has been described before can be thought of as a preface to theological reflection and construction. Do all of the steps in the process need to occur? Certainly not. But each of the elements in the process of moving from pastoral practice to theology have been helpful in the particular groups that I have supervised. The agenda for ministry groups can be shortened and adapted in a number of ways. However, too quick a move to theological reflection will result in a shallow or stereotypical formulation of theological ideas, something like the answers to catechetical questions. Put more simply, what comes out is simply not very interesting either to the one who presents it or to those who hear and respond to it.

Christian theology should be interesting. Alfred North Whitehead is remembered for his comment that it is important that a proposition be interesting as well as true. Theological ideas that are powerful in substance can be flat and dull when they are simply an afterthought, seen on one hand as obvious or on the other hand as unnecessary in describing a ministry event. Thus the group process and the theorizing about it are designed to capture the person and group in the theological enterprise, so that the ideas presented will have an interest and vitality comparable to the events that generated them.

The slowness in getting to reflection on specifically theological concepts also involves the bracketing process and the development of trust within the groups. Even with persons who have become comfortable and familiar with using theological language, an application of that language to one's own experience may appear on one hand to be presumptuous and on the other hand too personal for comfortable sharing. As suggested earlier, in speaking of the bracketing of theological material in the counseling process, it takes time to talk about these matters. Moreover, because theology grows out of the experience of a community of faith, one's involvement in that community requires that attention also be given to the perceptions and interpretations of others in the community as well as one's own. Theological formulation is not just an individual process. It is a process and product of engagement and dialogue with others.

This will become more evident in the forthcoming illustrative material.

The slowness of the theological reflection process is also preferred because the event presented for reflection is one in which the person may be deeply involved. This is not just "case material." It is a piece of a particular person's life. It cannot be discussed apart from the person who presents it. Thus ministry groups composed of students in CPE should present "old" material that they have already presented for supervision and looked at from the perspective of who they are as person and minister. Although they do not always respond in the way that I ask them, we do attempt to secure for reflection in the ministry groups events that, although examined before, still seem "unpacked" or full of meaning. For the lay groups less intensively involved in a long-term educational process, we expect simply that they bring in an event that is "meaning-full."

The Groups' Agenda

The structure and agenda for the ministry groups in this phase of the process is usually similar to the following:

Session nine. Sharing and responding to events that reveal the character of our ministry and contribute to what we understand ministry to be.

Session ten. Sharing and responding to pastoral events that are "meaning-full" and that may change or enrich our understanding of theological concepts other than ministry.

Session eleven. Theological consultation on how particular pastoral events may talk back to and enrich theology.

Session twelve. Sharing theological formulations growing out of pastoral events.

Self-Involvement in Theological Reflection

Elise did not want to present the verbatim, but she was accustomed to fulfilling requirements. The seminar's claim to be theological sometimes seemed offensive and at other times irrelevant to her training experience in ministry to the elderly. In seminary she had become comfortable discussing theology, and before that her experience as a nurse had acquainted her, if not made her comfortable, with the pain of human life. More than that, she had literally grown up in a nursing home. Her mother had operated one, and, as a child, Elise had worked and played among the patients there.

But the assignment was to bring in an event, a pastoral conversation with a patient or resident that seemed to be "meaning-full," one that was not obviously theological, in the sense of using religious or theological terms, but that nonetheless seemed to call for theological interpretation. Elise knew immediately the event that had been most "meaning-full" for her, but she did not particularly want to share it. In spite of that, and apparently only because she was expected to, she shared the following event:

> **Chaplain:** Hello, my name is Elise. I'm the chaplain here. I'd like to visit with you.
>
> **Resident:** You're the what?
>
> **Chaplain:** I'm a chaplain. I met you the other day.
>
> **Resident:** Where have I seen you before? I don't remember you. Have I seen you before?
>
> **Chaplain:** Yes, we met downstairs. The administrator introduced us.
>
> **Resident:** Oh, well. I don't remember. I've got a bad memory. You say you're the chaplain? I haven't met you before, have I?
>
> **Chaplain:** Yes, we walked together at the health center.
>
> **Resident:** I don't think I've ever met you. How long have you been here?
>
> **Chaplain:** I've been here since September. The administrator introduced us, and we walked together, but we've never really talked.
>
> **Resident:** You've been here since September? Why has it taken you so long to see me?
>
> **Chaplain:** (somewhat angrily) I'm here to see you *now*.

Chaplain Elise's event is a litany in which the minister expresses a variety of things and the congregation always answers with the same thing. But instead of the "Hear our prayer, O Lord," what is heard in this litany of pastoral care is "I don't know, I can't remember." During the long pause after the presentation the group seemed to be wondering as did I, "What is 'meaning-full' in this short repetitive interaction?" In the silence Elise seemed to be saying, "OK, I've presented it. See if you can make something theological out of it." Finally, after a long time, I said, "Elise, I'm feeling that you have presented something that is important and meaningful to you, but you have managed to leave the most important part out."

After suggesting to Elise that she had left out something, I ventured the interpretation that it may have had something to do with her rage at the situation in which her ministry and, perhaps, her life had placed her. I made no further interpretation of the resistance, which seemed to be saying, "I'll do what you say, turn in a verbatim. It's 'meaning-full' to me, but I dare you to find out why" or, to use the biblical symbol, "How can you ask me to sing a song of faith in a strange land? [Psalm 137] in a world where people are pushed out of the places that give their lives meaning?" I asked Elise if she would bring in the rest of the story the next time the seminar met. After some hesitation she said that she would.

When the group met again what Elise presented was still simple and in many ways unremarkable, but along with the empty litany of confusion and suppressed rage, there appeared a narrative, the story of a life and the experience of relationship. I share with you only a portion of what she shared with us.

"She's a lovely lady," began Elise as she told the story of the eighty-six-year-old retired social worker who talked of her trees and the view from the window of the place that she must leave because of her poor memory.

"I know they're not mine," the old woman said in her raspy soft voice, "but I like to think of them that way." She nodded her head the way the Indians are said to, and Elise thought of her own Native American heritage and soon learned of Ellen's. Ellen's Native American blood was Creek, from

South Georgia, near the great swamp Okefenokee. Elise's was Cherokee, from the foothills and mountains of the Appalachian range, whom my own nineteenth-century forefathers had sent on that long Trail of Tears to the arid plains of Oklahoma. What Elise had left out was the story and the relationship of these two part–Native American women, one young and one old, who learned to care for each other in spite of the different circumstances of their lives and the dying brain cells that caused one of them to forget.

But Elise could remember. She remembered Ellen sitting on her studio bed like a teenager at a spend-the-night party telling her of her home in South Georgia, a large, white, three-storied house at the cross roads. It had an attic and a front porch. "I grieve," said Elise, "that I have no magic phrase that will put her back in that house again. She seems calm and rational, but as the administrator comes again to tell her that she can't live here anymore, she has to move, I can feel her hurt, bewilderment, and sense of rejection. As I try to help her understand why this must be, my reasons seem pitiful and flimsy. And then I cried," Elise said.

"Are those tears for me?" Ellen asked. "For you and for me," Elise answered. "I don't think anyone ever cried for me before," Ellen said as she reached out to comfort Elise.

"I told her a story I was thinking of," said Elise, "of a time when I was rejected. It seemed silly and unimportant, but she handed me her tissues to wipe my eyes and seemed to feel happy comforting me.

"I have been with her many times since she moved," Elise concluded, "finding her in the lounge reading her *New York Times* or at church services in the building where she now lives."

"I think I know you," she said. "I don't remember, but I think I know you."

Many years ago, Seward Hiltner reminded us of the importance of what he called the ministry of sustaining—the tender, solicitous care that the pastor offers when no possibility of healing seems to exist.[1] The pastoral ministry of sustaining reminds us of the importance of going on, of offering ourselves in relationship when there can be no assurance of success. It may also bring us to be more in touch with ourselves through the awareness of our limits. And as theologians—from the psalmist who wondered how God could be aware of a human being (Psalm 8), down to the present time—have noted again and again how that awareness of our finitude and human limitation has pointed us to God.

Elise's resistance to sharing her event certainly had something to do with her as a person and where she was in her life, but it also illustrated the importance of the bracketing process. One does not quickly or easily share events and relationships in which one's self is involved. It takes encouragement from persons in a community where the sharp edge of critique has been blunted and where trust has developed to a significant degree. Theology that grows out of ministry events is attached to who one is as a human being. The construction or reconstruction of theology is an objectifying process, but that objectification proceeds slowly.

How was imagination involved in the reflection on this event? Clearly imagination was engaged as the ministry group allowed the event to resonate with the plight of the Hebrew people in Babylon—allowing the feelings related to the biblical event to express and interpret feelings associated with the "smaller" pastoral event. The group seemed to be aware that the two events could not naively be interpreted as the same, but they could speak to each other. And the lost identity of an old woman could clarify and enrich Elise's and the group's understanding of the relationship of place to who we are as persons and to the question of whether or not God has a place for us.

A Theology of Ministry

As I have observed and experienced it in groups of persons actively involved in and committed to ministry, there are inevitably two types of theology: a theology of ministry and a theology of everything other than ministry. When the issues of ministry are still so focused that other theological issues can only be dimly seen, a theology that grows out of pastoral practice is inevitably a theology of ministry—what ministry is, how it is possible, what authorizes it. When those issues begin to take shape, the person who presents the pastoral event and those who hear and respond to it can look away from the questions of what ministry is to other issues present in the material. One type of event is not better, more important, or more advanced than another type. The events are simply different.

In the pastoral event presented at the beginning of this book, Doug baptized the stillborn child with the tears of her parents and his own. In the group where he presented the event—his temporary community of faith—a number of theological issues emerged. Some had to do with the theology of baptism. What does baptism mean, and who is authorized to perform it? Does one have to be ordained? Is it appropriate to baptize the dead? The Christian traditions represented in the group generated different answers to those questions, and sometimes a particular group member's theology ("my theology") differed from the theology found in her or his tradition ("our theology"). Someone in the group commented that this was not really a baptism at all, it was merely a "naming" and a blessing. Whatever it was, the capacity of the event—even apart from the persons who directly experienced it—to stir human feelings and to understand it within the context of faith seems undeniable.

But when this event was shared in a ministry group, although a number of theological issues were discussed, the theology of ministry—more than any other theological issue—was the central focus of the discussion. As was the case when Doug first presented his event to his supervisor, the group dealt with the question of how Doug understood his own ministry. More important in this session, however, was what ministry meant to all of the group members and how it was understood in each of the Christian traditions that they represented.

Recall the event. Doug tried in vain to get a more experienced chaplain to come and officiate at the memorial service because he felt he did not know what to do. When he found no chaplain he quickly prepared some things to say. But when the nurse brought the stillborn baby into the chapel, Doug found that he could not say the things he had planned. "All I could do was stand there and cry." When the baby was presented for baptism, Doug acted intuitively. He brought his feelings and those of the parents together with the tradition of the church and its power to bless.

Someone in the group thought the event resonated with the question addressed to Jesus in the Synoptic Gospels, "By what authority are you doing these things?" (Matt. 21:23 RSV) I did not record the details of how Doug and the members of his ministry group struggled with that question. What I remember was that the event seemed, for all the group members, to focus on the questions of how ministry is possible, where the authority for ministry comes from, and how a person knows that one has it. Other theological issues were "there," but this one was so much in focus that the others could not be dealt with.

Another event that deals with the issues of authority for ministry and how ministry is possible, but that also points to other theological and social concerns, is the following one:

As I walked through the Medical Emergency Clinic I noticed a white male about sixty years old lying on a stretcher. I smiled at him and suddenly he looked at me and shouted, "Nigger, what are you smiling about?" Anger ripped through me as I turned away from him. I moved on to find more receptive patients, but I found myself unable to resist returning to him. I was unsure what either of us would say.

Chaplain: My name is Michael Moore, and I am the chaplain this afternoon. (Force a smile.) What brings you to us today?

Patient: (There seemed to be some confusion in his eyes.) What do you want with me?

Chaplain: (I think to myself, "That's a good question." I'm a little unsure myself. One part of me wants to cuss him out, but another part of me wants to know more about him.) I'm interested in how you are doing. (I ask myself, "Am I really?")

Patient: Hell, I can't be doing too good or I wouldn't be in here.

Chaplain: You sure seemed mad at somebody named "Nigger." What did he do to you?

Patient: (A sly smile appears on his face, and I wonder in my own mind what that means.) How do you know that I was not talking to you? (Still smiling.)

Chaplain: Because my name's not "Nigger." (The smile on his face changes, and I begin to feel a little more secure.) What brings you to the hospital?

Patient: Pain in my stomach. They say it's my liver, but it doesn't matter much anyway.

Chaplain: (I think he's an alcoholic. My anger begins to change to pity.) I don't understand. *What* doesn't matter?

Patient: (He looks away from me. When he turns back to me, he is looking very sad.) We've all got to die some time. You just don't know when or where. Besides, who cares? Nobody, that's who. Nobody cares about me, and I don't give a damn either. (His eyes are beginning to mist.)

Chaplain: You have no family? (And I think, "Uh-oh, here comes a little tear in the corner of his eye.")

Patient: I had a . . . (Then he doesn't say anything, and the tears are slowly rolling down his face. And I ask myself, "Why me?" Then I decide, "Oh well, here I go.")

Chaplain: You had a what?

Patient: (He turned away from me and wiped his tears.) I had a wife, but . . . (The tears start again. My own eyes begin to mist as he struggles to talk.) She run off with that . . .

Chaplain: Ran off with a black man?

Patient: (His tears are flowing pretty heavily and I feel his pain, and it hurts.) Yes, damn it. She ran off with that nig. . . . Excuse me, Chaplain, with that black SOB; and now I'm all alone. Why'd she have to do that to me? She just left a note saying good-bye. I loved her so much, and now look at me. What am I going to do?

Chaplain: (By now I'm a little shaky. I'm not sure what to do or say. Here comes the doctor, thank God.) I will try and get back to see you after the doctor leaves.

Patient: If you want to, okay.

Like Doug's event, Michael's also seems full of meaning. Because Michael seems to have handled a difficult situation well, there was in the group and, probably in those who respond to it now, a tendency to commend him on his ability to handle a difficult situation and let it go at that. Like Doug's event the dialogue in the emergency clinic elicited a good deal of feeling in Michael's group, but this time there was rage and pity as well as tenderness and compassion. The event seemed to say some things about the character of Christian ministry, but the group reflection went beyond that to issues of estrangement and reconciliation among groups of people, the meaning of individual and social destructiveness, and how faith might be relevant and irrelevant to the brokenness in individuals and society. When dealing with pastoral events, ministry concerns seem to have had first claim on both individual and community, but when those concerns have been addressed with some degree of adequacy, the community can move on to consider other theological and social concerns.

Theological Reflection in Theory

The kind of theological reflection that has taken place in the ministry groups appears to simulate what Edward Farley describes as "ecclesial reflection." Theological reflection, says Farley, is not so much "thinking about" as "an attempt to penetrate and open up matters which are present but hidden." He emphasizes further that this kind of reflection is "a continuing and at best partly successful enterprise, a reflection in process."[2]

Farley's view that theological reflection is not simply "thinking about" resonates with William James's contrast between "knowledge of" and "knowledge about," discussed in chapter 1. The reflection is not detached thinking about a distant object. It is an attempt to discover meaning in the world at hand, in what I have called the "meaning-full" events of life, particularly the events of ministry, in which the reflector or theologian has participated. Moreover, this kind of theological or ecclesial reflection, in my experience, as well as in Farley's theory, is at best only partly successful. As can be seen in the events presented in this chapter, it is a process that is never fully completed.

The source of theological reflection, according to Farley, is the world of everyday life: "the social and cultural world of values, intersubjective expectations, and the social past and future which is the immediate, taken-for-granted environment of every human being." It is in this world, not a special religious world, that faith occurs. In this ordinary world, "certain realities come to light, specific mutual intentionalities occur between human beings, and a special symbolic universe accompanies these activities."[3]

The following theological matters were perceived in the ministry groups when Michael, Elise, and Doug presented pastoral events: certain realities came to light (black/white racism between the old alcoholic and the young chaplain is not finally overcome, but temporarily bracketed out by one's need for pastoral care and the other's commitment to ministry); specific mutual intentionalities occur between human beings (Elise and Ellen find that their similarities are more powerful than their differences, their understanding of each other more persuasive than their estrangement); and a special symbolic universe accompanies these activities (Doug's ministry, which called for a memorial service at the end of life, parabolically is transformed into a call for a baptism to begin Christian life.)

There is something in the faith-world, continues Farley, which grounds it, unifies it, influences it, and which is the primary reference of faith. Theological reflection, as we are discussing it here, does not move first to Christian tradition's presentation of the nature of God. It begins with the ordinary world of life that calls for a God and, by the specific character and need of that world, for a God with particular attributes. It does not ignore the tradition. As an ecclesial or faith community the tradition is part of its life and assumptive world, but the reflective method, which Farley describes and which I have experienced in the ministry groups, begins with ministry event rather than with thinking about God. Farley insists, as do I, that the dynamics in the reflective process are neither self-analysis on one hand nor acceptance of the authority of the church on the other. As an action of an ecclesial community, however, it does occur "in a specific context, the breaking of the power of human evil" and thus occurs "as a response to the Adamic-Gospel story." And it sometimes involves "worship, repentance, trust, and belief."

Farley's goal is the transformation of theology "from judgments as citations of authorities to judgments as truth-intending expressions of realities."[4] My goal is considerably more modest and more practical, but it is consistent, I believe, with the three dimensions that Farley identifies in his method.

The first dimension, "the symbolic universe of ecclesiality," he says, may be understood as looking at existence within the ecclesial community, which is "an actual historical community pervaded by a dominant story, the Adamic-Gospel story." The concern here is with understanding the central themes of the story with respect to internal consistency and relationship to one another. In the ministry groups the effort toward understanding the Gospel themes comes not in didactic instruction, nor in systemic reading of traditional sources, but in consultation about the events presented and relating them to the group's understanding of their tradition. (The person presenting an event should be encouraged to explore the literature of his or her tradition on a particular theological theme, but there is no common theological curriculum for study.)

The second dimension of theology, according to Farley, "the universal dimension," brings ecclesial existence in relation to wider fields of evidence, relating the Gospel story and its claims of universal relevance to other views of the human being in the world by using some kind of correlational method. Ecclesial reflection submits what is before it "to formal, rational criteria of internal consistency, the external consistency with other realms of factuality, and to considerations raised by universal ontological accounts of being and knowledge."[5] The themes of the Gospel are understood in some ways to be universal; therefore they must be related to other views of human being, the world, God, and the relationships between them. This dimension of theology often appears in relating the ministry events to psychological or cultural theories of person and situation. The presenter of the event may be referred to the work of a particular, not specifically theological theorist (for example, Leslie Stevenson's *Seven Theories of Human Nature* or Paul Pruyser's *Changing Views of the Human Condition*[6]) for ways to interpret what he or she has experienced and to enrich the understanding of the event delivered in dialogue through the theological symbol.

The third dimension of theology is a move back from the general to the specific—"the concreteness of individual and social, contemporary situations. This dimension brings forward and draws upon the first two dimensions." Here "the theologian interrogates, attempting by the retention of the first two dimensions as criteria to insightfully grasp the problematics and possibilities of the situation."[7] This dimension characterizes rather well the primary focus of the ministry groups' experience in reflecting on pastoral events—"interrogating" the pastoral event in order that it might speak more clearly to the theological and other conceptualizations that have been brought into the situation.

The product of theological reflection, according to Farley, is "theological portraiture," a metaphor that characterizes theology less like a photograph than an impressionistic painting. Like a painting, a theological portrait has discrete identifiable elements in it. Some elements are explicitly theological symbols, for example, hope, evil, and the eternal. Other elements are more generic, involving symbols like time, place, and the relationships of generations. And the elements in the picture, whatever they are, "exist in some sort of relationship to each other." "One might say they form a landscape. These relations are not simply created by interpretation, for the elements are given originally as being related to each other."[8]

Like all metaphors, however, this one has limits, the most serious of which is that it, like any painting, "brings reality to a stop," whereas reality is in "perpetual change, being reformed as the individual's worldly and ecclesial discernments and experiences occur."[9] Both the characterization of theology as being like a painting and as being an image of the temporary cessation of reality in the face of perpetual change are useful expressions of the ministry groups' experience. The theology that comes out of the dialogue is pointed and sometimes gripping, but inexact. It temporarily stops the thinking of both the presenter and the consultative group, and that stop is necessary in order to gain commitment to a way of thinking and symbolizing. But the process is incomplete, a fact symbolized in the groups I have led by my having no expectation of a "final" paper on the theological concept explored. The following event may not be what Farley means by "theological portraiture," but it is a powerful portrait of the question of humanity in one who is broken and those whose task it is to deal with his brokenness.

Theological Reflection in Practice

As I entered the surgical emergency clinic one of the male nurses recognized me and said, "Chaplain, I think they could use you in the first treatment room. There's a guy in there who really needs some prayer. He got beat up pretty bad." When I came into the room I saw an older man lying on the stretcher. He was lying calmly, but mumbling to himself. He was apparently drunk. His head and face were swollen and covered with blood. His cheek bone was crushed, and the eye on that side appeared to have been destroyed. His head looked to me like a Halloween mask, so gross, so distorted, so eerie. It looked like he should be dead, but there he was talking to himself, an odd reminder that he was very much alive.

Chaplain: What happened to him?

Nurse: Someone beat him with a lead pipe.

Chaplain: How did it happen?

Nurse: We don't know. The firemen just said that a man came to the station and reported that he had just beaten a guy and told them where he was. He had the pipe in his hand.

Chaplain: What would cause one human being to beat another like that?

Nurse: Hey, there's a lot of crazy people out there.

As I stood there, several doctors came in to look at this broken, beaten man. Because of his many injuries, several services were represented: ophthalmology, neurology, plastic surgery, and others. It appeared that each hoped the other would admit him and take responsibility. Eventually plastic surgery took him, but reluctantly because they wanted the trauma service to take him. Although he was quite conscious, they stood over him and gaped, talking about him as if he were not there. I realized that I had been doing the same thing.

Doctor: Do we have a chart on him?

Nurse: We don't know his name. He may have been here before, but we don't know.

I wondered who this nameless person was and went over to him and lightly stroked his arm. Immediately he erupted in rage, cursing and telling me to leave him alone.

> **Chaplain:** Sir, I'm the chaplain here. I don't want to hurt you. You are in the county hospital. We're here to help you. Can you tell us your name?

He garbled something, and after several tries we could finally understand him. The nurse entered the name in the computer and found that he had a hospital record.

> **Nurse:** Thanks, Chaplain, I didn't think we would get a name on him.

A surgery resident came in and began to sew up a wound in his hand. As I stood watching him work, I wondered who this man was. What was his story? Somewhere he had been a child. He had had a mother and a father. I wondered what his life had been like. There were other scars on his head. This was probably not his first fight. I looked at the clock. It was 2:00 A.M. I was tired, and I decided to go upstairs and try to sleep.

The following is an abbreviated version of the group's response and consultation to the presenter of the event.

> (After a rather lengthy silence)

> **Group Leader:** What did you notice? What did you feel?

> **First Group Member:** Doctors and residents have to do their technical work with things like this, and they lose their feelings.

> **Second Group Member:** (breaks in) But if it were someone they knew by name. . . .

> **Third Group Member:** They would act real different.

> **Second Group Member:** As you were reading this my temperature was rising.

Fourth Group Member: I just couldn't believe that they didn't give any kind of pain killer to the guy.

Group Member Who Presented the Event: (angrily) They were literally putting their fingers in his wounds.

First Group Member: But if you have someone who you don't know how much he's drunk, you have to be careful with medication.

Group Leader: I find myself thinking of identity and care or lack of it, the pushing away of care by the patient, whatever that means. "Don't mess with me," he said cursing. The namelessness, the disfigurement and distortion of his human being. I suppose there was loss of himself in the drunkenness even before the beating happened.

Presenting Group Member: Nameless, sightless. The thing that struck me was the propheticness of being a pastor at times. I found myself wondering if Amos or Isaiah would have stood silent as I did while this man was treated like an object. My guess is that they would have hopped up on one of the stretchers and started preaching or something. It felt like I had abdicated a prophetic opportunity. I was angry about my silence.

First Group Member: But you stepped in when he was cursing the doctors and nurses, walked up and touched him and asked him his name. You moved the medical people aside to ask what needed to be known—who he was.

Second Group Member: There was some dignity in his cursing and his anger, in not wanting to be messed with.

Presenting Group Member: "Don't poke at me when I'm lying here sightless and helpless." That was powerful.

Group Leader: I think you're on to something.

Third Group Member: There are some Psalms like that.

First Group Member: And the book of Job.

Group Leader: Even in the hospital where you claim your place by what's wrong with you, nobody wanted this man. He was even homeless there.

Presenting Group Member: I guess the most pastoral thing I did was to get his name.

Group Leader: You recognized something there beyond the disfigurement and self-destruction, your own anger and helplessness about what was happening. The simple seeking of the name in the midst of all that negative stuff seems to me to have a lot of meaning. In baptizing an infant, you say, "Name this child," or something like that. Is there still a Christian name for somebody like this?

Presenting Group Member: I now remember what made me think of his having been a child. We also had to get his birthdate. I didn't get that in what I wrote up. We had to have his birthdate to find him in the computer. This person was born. He was a baby.

That is a specific example of at least a portion of the theological reflection that occurred in response to this pastoral event. If we consider it in the light of the discussion of theological reflection that preceded it, how does what actually happened in this situation fit with the theory? Theological reflection, as I described it following Farley, is not just "thinking about." It is an attempt "to penetrate and open up matters which are present but hidden." The group's reaction is like that. It is not simply dispassionate thinking clearly separated from the event. The event has claimed involvement and demanded response, perhaps even from the reader. Is the drunken, cursing, sightless man human? Are the doctors discussing who will have to be responsible for him any more or less human? Each reveals his or her brokenness and stirs up the possibility of self-righteousness and a claim of difference in those who listen and stand by.

The group is responding to what Farley called "the social and cultural world of values, intersubjective expectations, and the social past and future which is the immediate, taken-for-granted environment of every human being." It is not a religious world; it is a brutal, everyday world. But even here "certain realities come to light, specific mutual intentionalities occur between human beings, and a special symbolic universe accompanies these activities." In reality the patient has no name and history—without identity there is detachment, chaos, and confusion. The chaplain secures his name and the symbolic universe is reactivated for all involved.

This type of theological reflection does not begin with God but with a specific character and need of the world, which calls for a God with particular attributes—a God who can still care for human beings who reveal their character in an event like the one presented above. The "Adamic" part of what Farley calls the "Adamic-Gospel story" is quite evident, as well as the question of whether in this context it is indeed possible to break "the power of human evil." Although it is only a fragmentary symbol, the chaplain's asking for and discovery of name, his asking for and discovery of a birthdate make this man into a person with a history. The chaplain's own reflection on what he has left out of the written report is instructive. He had forgotten about the birthdate as the key to finding the patient's history, and the birthdate allows him to see that the broken human figure was once an unspoiled child with a mother. The chaplain helped to name him, just as the church helps to give us a Christian name.

Most of what has been given in the group's consultation represents the first step in the reflective method that I have described—penetrating into the hidden dimensions of the event. The next steps, which Farley describes as the three dimensions of theology, are begun in associating the chaplain's questions about his behavior in the event in relation to the prophet Amos and in relating naming to personhood, both in the secular sphere and in the world of faith. The third step, not taken here, would be interpreting the religious symbols, doctrinal formulations, and what has been revealed through the event, in order to move toward "theological portraiture." Thus, if the process moves along as it should, the broken, sightless man and the broken, symbolically sightless physicians may contribute to some new vision of human existence in relation to God.

The Hermeneutical Circle

Is it really possible for events to speak to and to change our theological understanding? When looking at the fields of both practical and philosophical theology, one wonders if the pastoral event just discussed is really available to us, or do we have only the various interpretations of it. In reading the literature of practical theology today, it appears that the interpretation of the living human document has become more important than the document itself. The "nerve" of the pastoral theological method of Anton Boisen and his followers may have already been "cut," and what we have been doing here may have become only an interesting exercise no longer relevant for theology and ministry.

The so-called hermeneutical perspective makes us, who are committed to the clinical method of theological education, aware of our naive assumption that it is simple to move from experience to theology. The emphasis on hermeneutics has made us aware that there is a rather sophisticated process that goes on when we take our pastoral experience with theological seriousness and that there are significant problems involved in gaining access to our experience. I touch on only two crucial barriers.

The first problem might be called the loss of the object or the loss of human confidence that the objective world, as we experience it, is accessible to us at all. Immanuel Kant's philosophy moved God from the object of our experience to a necessary presupposition for our moral experience. A concept of God, reasoned Kant, is required for human moral experience to be meaningful and is a presupposition that is required in order to make sense of things. Although we cannot experience God objectively, we can affirm that God is involved in the general consciousness or experience of human beings. Much of modern theology can be related to the impact of Kant's thought concerning this turning inward to think about God, instead of looking outward.

The second problem is also related to the availability of experience but more specifically to the effect of language. Any experience is shaped by the language we use to describe it; therefore what we are dealing with is not the experience itself but with the language and the hermeneutical or interpretive process used to communicate it. Thus modern theology becomes not only a theology limited by human experience and consciousness but also a theology confined by its language. Not so much the content of theology, its doctrines and documents, but the way theology is done—its method—becomes a theory of interpretation or hermeneutics.

The problem is framed by using the words of philosopher Nancy Frankenberry: "Experience is conditioned and limited by the language which is at once both the instrument of expression and largely also the conditioning medium of experience itself." It becomes extremely difficult, therefore, "to signify to what extent language is a distillation or a distortion of experience, or to what entent the experience is a function of and determined by the available forms of language."

This complex relationship between qualitative experience and linguistic expression, says Frankenberry, plunges us into a hermeneutical circle that is nearly impossible to escape.[10] If this is in fact the case, how can we do theological reflection on pastoral events? If those events are already caught in a language system that must be "hermeneutically waded through" before we can approach the event that seems "meaning-full," how can we respect and recover our experience in the light of the limits of human consciousness in apprehending events and of the limits of human language in describing them?

Although she does not develop it, philosopher Frankenberry suggests a way out of this hermeneutical circle. She concludes that the "distinctive objectivity of the datum of experience exerts its own subtle checks upon our socially mediated sign-systems." She points to the limits of language and interpretation identified by Wittgenstein and James. According to Wittgenstein:

> Some things can be said about the particular experience and besides this there seems to be something, the most essential part of it, which cannot be described. . . . As it were: there is something further about it, only you *can't say* it; you can only make the general statement. It is this idea which plays hell with us. (Notes for Lectures on Private Experience and Sense-Data)

What James said was this: the concepts we talk with are made for purposes of *practice* and not for purposes of *insight*. . . . I must *point,* point to the mere *that* of life, and you by inner sympathy must fill out the *what* for yourselves.[11]

How do Wittgenstein and James help us out of our entrapment within a circle of interpretation, which suggests that rather than responding to event and experience we are only responding to our own words? They remind us of the limits of our words and interpretations and, in effect, warn us not to take them too seriously. As Wittgenstein says, there is something in experience that "cannot be described." It is clear that there is no such thing as uninterpreted experience or a simple consultation of experience. Yet event and experience effect theory and observations modify interpretations as well as the other way around, and that is important to affirm. Although we cannot escape the circle of our interpretations, the event is still there, questioning the adequacy of our interpretations. Language and interpretation are not all there is.

Philosopher Paul Ricoeur develops this view: "Language is not a world of its own. It is not even a world. But because we are in the world, because we are affected by situations, and because we orient ourselves comprehensively in those situations, we have something to say, we have experience to bring to language."[12] The effect of language, which is used to describe experience, can be illustrated by contrasting the meaning of metaphor and symbol. "Metaphor occurs in the already purified universe of the *logos,* while the symbol hesitates on the dividing line between *bios* and the cosmos." A metaphor "is a free invention of discourse; the symbol is bound to the cosmos. . . . In the sacred universe the capacity to speak is founded upon the capacity of the cosmos to signify. Metaphor is just a linguistic procedure within which symbolic power is deposited. . . . symbols in contrast. . . . plunge their roots into the durable constellations of life, feeling, and the universe." The symbol is bound to reality and experience. It communicates that reality, but cannot change or negate it.[13]

One of my teachers, Bernard Meland, used the phrase "appreciative awareness" to describe an openness to the data of this non-semantic world that allows those data to speak and disclose a pattern of meaning. The "realities of faith" transpire within lived experience as perceptual events and are known consciously in "appreciative awareness." Although he acknowledges that it is questionable whether experience is prior to conceptualization in every act of cognition, Meland, an intellectual heir of William James, asserts that there is a primal disparity between language and reality. Perception is a "thicker experience" than conceptualization. For Meland there is a depth dimension of lived experience involving much more than we are explicitly and articulately conscious of. The ultimate can be experienced in the present.[14] Ultimacy is an aspect of immediacy that affirms the relational ground of every event. Grace and all other theological concepts or realities are resources emanating from relationships within the context of this lived experience.[15]

As a part of their excellent summary of the basic features of an empirical and phenomenological method applicable for practical theology, Poling and Miller also emphasize the importance of being in touch with experience as well as our interpretations of it. Life, they say, "is a constant dialectic of immersion in experience and distancing from it." The "danger of the reflective process is the impoverishment of the richness of experience. . . . All abstractions, including theology, must be held tentatively and self-critically, and must continually be tested against experience in its depth."[16] With this understanding of the limits of our access to the events of life *and* of the limits of theology and any other language system to give them adequate conceptualization, I return to the experience of the ministry groups.

The Second Round of Reflection and Consultation

The first round of theological reflection in practice is sharing and responding to pastoral events that are "meaning-full" and may change or enrich our understanding of theological concepts other than ministry. This process is illustrated with the event of the man with no name. Now I examine what happens the second time an event is presented. Perhaps the process would be clearer if I were to stay with the same event, but unfortunately the second discussion of that event was not recorded. This new event, however, may in some ways be more useful because, in contrast to the powerfully impacting event in the emergency clinic, this one is singularly unremarkable but equally rewarding for theological reflection. The presenter has taken the response of the group to the first presentation of the material, reflected on it, and put together another presentation in the light of it. As was the case before, the material has been abbreviated and summarized.

The group member who had presented it began by summarizing what he had shared before:

My pastoral event, you may remember, was with a sixty-six-year-old woman who was born in West Germany and who lived most of her adult life in the United States and was in the psychiatric unit of the hospital when I visited her. She had given me her life story, a very lengthy, difficult, hurtful kind of story. When we talked about it in the group before, we worked on the idea that telling a hurtful story can help the person get beyond it, but in this case it seemed like she had told this story many times and was still not beyond it. I began to play with the idea of why this wasn't helping, and picking up on something that was mentioned in the group—the laments in the Old Testament—I looked back at some of the things that Walter Brueggemann had done. As I looked at that, what became most evident to me were some of the differences between this woman's story and the lament Psalms.

One of the things Brueggemann says is that the lament Psalms are not only a rehearsal of a hurtful story but they most always imply that Yahweh should do something about it.[17] Such and such has happened, so do something about it. There is a moving beyond the self. That got me to thinking about that difference. As I looked back on her story, it seemed that she was not able to disconnect her story from herself enough to lay it in someone else's lap. She was at a place where she felt responsible for everything that had happened. There was a shame about what had happened that she had taken on herself and left there. She was so ashamed that she could not divorce it from herself.

The lament Psalms are different. They don't just take it. They say, "Look at these bad people, God; get 'em." She was not able to say that about her father or her stepmother. That's the edge of something for me. It made me think of Gordon Kaufman's idea of God as whatever is beyond the limits of the world.[18] Because there are limits in the world, we need to posit the concept of God. If we don't feel any limits to what we are responsible for, we are stuck with a world that is the whole of things. That seemed to be what she was in. In the Psalms there's my world, but there's a limit to my world and my responsibilities. People in the Psalms are able to say, "This is what I am not responsible for." Brueggemann makes a lot out of Israel's being able to hold God accountable for whatever is beyond what they perceive to be the limits of their responsibility.

Group Leader: You were able to use this method to move beyond where you were. You were bringing this woman into dialogue with Brueggemann and the Psalms, noting their similarities and differences. You held them together loosely, letting them speak to each other informally, and then looked for a theoretical or theological way to make some more sense of the dialogue. That's where you brought in Kaufman and the business of limits as we experience the world.

First Group Member: This is an interesting way to look at the purpose of ministry—to help the people disengage enough from their world to acknowledge the limits of it and look beyond.

Group Leader: That's a pastoral care theory intersecting with theology. One of the functions of the minister is to help a person see that she is not the only one, to do a kind of objectifying.

Presenting Group Member: It's interesting to me personally because I have thought of pastoral care as a very subjective kind of endeavor—feelings and that kind of thing. But I can see now a very strong component of objectivizing—a moving out from self enough so that you can get in touch with yourself.

Second Group Member: She wanted to keep it herself or couldn't put it outside to let God get 'em—to say, "You take care of it now."

Third Group Member: It makes me think of the tension I pick up from Kaufman between the real world and the world that we have imagined. She's not able to distinguish between reality and imagination. And I think all of us are something like that.

Group Leader: Isn't there a social parallel to the theological one, an oppressed group, taking all responsibility and then angrily putting it outside themselves—a turning outward. The next step, I think, is coming up with a balance between what is mine and what is not mine.

Presenting Group Member: Perhaps there's something specific about marginalized groups that allows them to do what the laments do. If you're in the majority, you have the anxiety that Tillich talks about because there's no real threat you can put your finger on, so you become internally anxious, and it's harder to say, "It's not my fault."

Group Leader: Marginalized groups have a way of speaking the truth without having to worry about what the truth might cost them.

Second Group Member: The marginalized are free because the pain is expected. We're going to be hurt regardless of what we say or do.

Third Group Member: In the experience of black people, the plight is a common plight, and the community is the pastoral care giver, helping to objectify. Black people visualize themselves as the remnant.

First Group Member: To go back to the event and her questioning whether she believes in God anymore, it's like the laments and their questioning whether God's out there. She may be able at least a little bit to objectify, using you to get her out of herself.

Third Group Member: Even to ask the question is to affirm something about God's being out there.

This second round of reflection is different because the presenter has brought his event into specific dialogue with the Christian tradition as he has studied it and heard about it from his colleagues. He uses specific theological ideas to interpret his pastoral event. The process is far from complete, but this incident from the group shows some of the ways that theological reflection takes place and is facilitated by others.

Theological Play

The possibility of getting lost in the hermeneutical circle is not the only danger that inhibits theological reflection. Consider also the usually hidden assumption that only professional theologians do good theology. Another inhibition is the critical spirit growing out of our various insecurities and encouraged by the belief that we must be right at all costs. Facilitated by the bracketing process, the development of community substitutes acceptance for correctness and allows us to use our imaginations to play with the theological formulations of our faith rather than simply attempt to conform to them. Theology needs the experiences of life and care for others to challenge and oppose both its hasty conceptualizations and its rigidities.

The method described in this book was developed before I discovered James Whitehead's article "The Practical Play of Theology." "Theological reflection in ministry," Whitehead notes, always entails an

> imaginative interplay of authorities. Effective and enjoyable interplay happens only if these authorities really engage one another. If tradition overwhelms a person's experience with its interpretation, no interplay occurs; likewise, if one's experience is so absorbing that it ignores or rejects any information from the religious tradition, no exchange happens.[19]

Whitehead also notes the interplay of the authorities with the imagination. "Our deepest convictions and biases abide not in clear and available intellectual concepts, but in the images and fantasies often hidden somewhere within us." He takes Erik Erikson's concept of play as "testing the leeway," and John Dominic Crossan's concept of play as "disciplined failure," and applies them to the interplay between tradition and our experience. "It is precisely in the leeway between the old and the new, the traditional and contemporary experience, that we play our lives."[20] In that kind of process we say who we are. He suggests that the practical play of theology involves three phases: the leap of delight; the move against gravity (testing the leeway); and coming back down to earth, learning to fall.

His "leap of delight" can be identified as the "meaning-full" event and the awareness one has of its importance and value. "Testing the leeway" is similar to "talking back" to the religious tradition, seeing in one's event a way to change what one has received from tradition. Whitehead's returning to earth or learning to fall involves what I have often referred to as the "messiness of pastoral theology." Event and theological conceptualization never fit exactly with each other. The results of the interplay are never fully satisfactory, and the process of "talking back" to one's tradition is usually more important for its having been done than for what it produces.

Whitehead, nevertheless, emphasizes the importance of this process as he notes that it "is neither an emergency maneuver nor a temporary burden in Christian life; it *is* our life, how we do, who we are. It is in such activities that we identify ourselves and imagine our religious tradition's future."[21] He affirms theologically that "creation is still being played" and that what is done in the theological reflection of ministry groups is part of that play. If we can be aware of that, he says,

> we may be encouraged to get better at playing. Only by playing more gracefully will we recover its delight. Some delight returns as we recall that these "contests" between tradition and experience are affairs of intimacy. We engage our religious tradition when we wrestle Jacoblike with some part of Scripture or our denominational history.[22]

Action and Interpretation in Pastoral Event

Theologian Anne Carr, basing much of what she says on the work of Karl Rahner, argues that religious truths received in the Christian tradition can also be discerned in contemporary life. "The patterns of grace and revelation illumined in an extraordinary and exceptional fashion in the Scriptures are also visible, to the disciplined observer, in our own lives." Human experience does not simply receive from Christian tradition in a passive way; "it is transformed in dialogue with this Tradition." "Experience," says Carr, "demands to be heard for its own information concerning the interplay of a person and a community with the Holy. Because human experience is already open to the gracious activity of God, it, along with the Tradition, could be a genuine source for theologizing. . . . Each would be a corrective of the other."[23]

Julie's experience, to use Carr's words, "demands to be heard." "I will never forget this pastoral event," Julie wrote, "not because I did marvelous ministry with these people but because in spite of, and maybe even through, my ineptitude and their open grief we connected, and something of the real stuff of life and ministry took place."

> I was called down to the pediatric I.C.U. where a mother and father were crying over their eighteen-month-old child who was in renal failure. I stood with them, comforted them while they cried, and then prayed with them, but as the prayer ended the mother turned to me and said hysterically, "I need someone to tell me about Jesus."
>
> I didn't know what to say. What could I say about Jesus at that moment that would not sound trite? How could anything I said match their pain as the beautiful child lay there dying? Apparently exasperated by my silence, the mother made a second request. "Would you sing to me, would you sing 'Jesus Loves Me'?" As I held her I began singing "Jesus Loves Me." Her husband came up to the baby's bed, held his wife from the other side and stroked the baby's leg as he joined in singing his version of "Jesus Loves Me," which was "Jesus Loves *You*" to the baby. With all my theological training and course work, no preplanning could have created the power of that event. It was in the spontaneity of the moment when we were all connected in our grief and helplessness that something beyond us entered in and the real stuff of ministry took place.

Julie's ministry in the pediatric I.C.U. was for her "meaning-full," but how is it theological? Most obviously, it contributes to a theology of ministry. This is where pastoral experience and theology are first related to each other. This is the assumption of clinical pastoral education, and most theological reflection in CPE has to do with a theology of ministry. The clinical method looks at the act of ministry, examines it for what it reveals about the particular minister involved, and then asks the question of how this particular event may contribute to the understanding of what Christian ministry is, as well as what it is for Julie. It may say something about the relevance and power of speechlessness in the presence of human pain, about the regression to a childlike faith, and an openness to one's need that demands that Julie sing when she does not feel like singing. Experience in ministry that seems "meaning-full" always says something theological about what ministry is, almost convincing even the most rigid of us that a theology of ministry is never complete, always open-ended. With ministry something new can be said continually. Pastoral experience "talks back" to theology and enriches it.

But what of the rest of theology—the doctrines of God, Christ, the Holy Spirit, salvation, eschatology, and the like? What does speechlessness and singing say to these more firmly entrenched and less experientially assailable concepts? Julie's reflection was, "When we were all connected in our grief and helplessness . . . something beyond us entered in." Where two or three are gathered together in Jesus' name—singing "Jesus Loves You" to a dying child—there is some kind of divine presence, or wholeness. The relationship is completed with the Holy Spirit. Love and care seem to be present when human care has failed to save. There is life and vitality in the midst of pain. Is the God who is with us a suffering God, one who has waited patiently unable to change the course of things as God's child dies? Is God like the human threesome who stood singing at the bed, broken and helpless as they stood alone, but who seemed to be able to act together when neither individual could act alone?

What am I doing with Julie's event? What did the listening faith community do with it? I and they let the event move from the "first floor of experience" where it took place, up through the second floor of the imagination, and there let the imagination "play," or roam freely, saying, like the T.V. commercial, "What if?" or like the nine- or ten-year-old kids, "Hey, let's let God be like . . ." "Maybe God's not like this, but like that." What this and other pastoral events suggest to us is that theology is not to be memorized like a creed or memorialized like an icon. Human imagination enlivened by divine creativity suggests that it may be handled like a toy or a game to see what it will do, to discover its limits. The problem with most theology is that we leave it alone and don't "test the leeway," explore alternatives—play with it.

After this time of imagining, of playing with the event and where it may point theologically, there is a time of association with remembered theological ideas and books or articles. The group leader asks Julie what she thinks she might want to explore theologically, if she goes "back to the books." She answers, and the group members and leaders act as consultants by suggesting to her how she might explore a particular area of theology—a Bible dictionary's view of the Holy Spirit and how it compares to what happened in the ministry event, Jürgen Moltmann's view of the Trinity, or process theology's view of a relational God. A period of time goes by while other group members share their events and Julie does her "homework." Then she again presents to the group, reminding them of the event but focusing on what she has done in her more traditional theological exploration. It is a progress report on the dialogue between her event and the part of the Christian tradition she has examined and re-examined. She may or may not move from there to the writing of a paper or a sermon on her area of theology. That's up to her. More important, she and the other members of the group have had practice in the process of doing imaginative theology informed by the events of ministry.

Pastoral theology can never have quite the organized and finished quality or the systematic presentation of doctrinal theology because it is in relation to an ongoing ministry. Its final product usually seems in-process and unfinished. Nevertheless, it does require time, a community of ministers actually committed to and involved in ministry, and some degree of belief in the importance of using the imagination in theological formulation. To some degree these things are required of all theology, but they are essential for pastoral theology.

Julie concluded the write-up of her ministry with the sentence: "I didn't create the power of that event, and being vulnerable means I can't control the way God will choose to minister through me, and that, though frightening, is exciting." Letting our pastoral events speak to our theology is also exciting—and after all, the excitement about what had happened to them motivated the apostles to begin the Christian church.

Reflections on the Process

After looking back on the experience of being in the ministry groups, the group members described what happened in this way:

Foundationally, we asked the question: What is it about our experience as human beings (and our reflection on that experience) that leads us to make theological assertions. We began with ourselves and moved toward theological statements about God. The word *we* has been important to our understanding of this process, for community enables us to do this task with integrity.

Several things stand out as I reflect on what happened in the group. The first was the diversity of the group, which prevented a one-sided theological reflection. Second, in the midst of that diversity, the same themes kept emerging from all the stories, for example, separation, leaving, and coming home. It appears that from very different contexts and cultures many of the same human themes and experiences occur. This commonality makes it more nearly possible to relate *our* story to *the* story. My story holds meaning not only for me but also for the community involved in the reflective process. In fact, my story can be a beginning point for the community to explore new insights about the meaning of God. Third, the process of telling our stories helped us to recover them. We discovered new meaning in our stories as we heard others respond to them, and it was meaning that seemed important enough to allow us to think theologically about things that at first seemed too simple to bother with.

I found that the group's theologizing helped broaden my experience, yet at the same time allowed me to keep ownership of my experience even as it contributed to a larger and somewhat more general or systematic plane of theological thought. I particularly liked what one member of the group said about the group's story becoming part of his story. I would add that his story is also now a part of the group's story. It is this kind of reciprocal dynamic that I found most exciting about our process and its implications for the interrelatedness of each of our stories with the Christian story.

Epilogue

I come to the end of this book reminded of my second favorite quotation from William James (the first is about the crab's outrage at being classified as a crustacean). Commenting on the unlikelihood that the truth of a proposition will be neatly related to the evidence for it, James writes, "In the great boarding-house of nature the cakes and the butter and the syrup seldom come out so even and leave the plates so clean."[1]

This book is a bit like that. There are a number of topics left over and not cleaned up. The most obvious is the relationship of the book's thesis and the data that are used to support it. I have said that theology is a product of the imagination creatively stirring the elements of the faith tradition with our contemporary experience of ministry. Although that way of putting it suggests the image of a bowl in which faith tradition and contemporary experience are stirred together by the "spoon" of imagination, I have tried to factor out the primary elements stirred together by using the image of a pyramid. Imagination, which I affirm theologically to be a part of both human and divine creativity, fills the pyramid, touching each of its base points. These points reach up toward and are, in fact, connected to the ultimate or, theologically stated, God. God touches the base points: action, relationship, and meaning through the imagination or through human creativity that has been empowered by divine creativity.

Assertions about the importance of the imagination in

theological construction are not new or unusual, although they have been less frequent in practical or pastoral theology. What I have said here is similar in a number of ways to one of the more recent studies of theology and the imagination, Garrett Green's *Imagining God: Theology and the Religious Imagination*. Simply stated, imagination, according to Green, is what revelation speaks to. Conceiving of "the point of contact between divine revelation and human experience in terms of imagination allows us to acknowledge the priority of grace in the divine-human relationship while at the same time allowing its dynamics to be described in analytical and comparative terms as a human religious phenomenon."[2]

In contrast to Green's work, I have only touched on the nature of imagination in a theoretical way. I have, however, illustrated its use in the events and responses to them of members of the ministry groups. What I think has been fairly clear is how imaginative sharing of the events of one's life can contribute to the development of community. Community, in turn, "stands" between event and interpretation—between action and meaning, facilitating the recall and celebration of an event, and inhibiting premature interpretation of it. Moreover, although shared events belong primarily to the persons who share them, their interpretation is not simply an individual one but grows out of community. The discovery of meaning through interpretation, however, is not an end in itself. Theological reflection, through community, leads back to pastoral action.

I have argued that not only does the creative center of the pyramid facilitate relationship between the points on the base, but also that the relationship of those points facilitates creativity, imagination, and the move toward the pyramid's apex, the ultimate, God. Both the faith traditions that group members have brought to their new community of faith—the ministry group—and their actions in ministry can be viewed imaginatively because of the acceptance of the community. This acceptance enables and encourages the process of theological reflection on the events of ordinary life and of ministry.

Reflection and sharing in the community of ministers validates the members of that community as persons who can risk handling the faith and interpreting it in the light of their experience. These meanings, shared in relationship with other members of the community of ministers, contributes to the life of that community and, sometimes, to the larger community of faith to which the members are accountable. The new imaginatively informed interpretation and the experience of the community that has helped create it encourages and empowers the members to continue their ministries and to engage the pain and possibility of the human situation more creatively.

The process of theological reflection is one in which brackets—like those described in phenomenology—are imposed early in a group's experience together and then within the context of a developing community gradually removed. I have suggested that a similar method is appropriate in pastoral care and counseling. Theological ways of conceptualizing life experiences are best deferred until a significant relationship and language appropriate to that relationship are developed. Removing the brackets too soon results in a theology that seems merely to be slapped onto an experience rather than one that naturally grows out of it and cautiously interprets it. To return to the pyramid image, one approaches the ultimate slowly or speaks about the distant apex only with a great deal of help from the imagination.

Even with that kind of statement of caution, I am concerned about a glib optimism with respect to human-divine connection that the pyramid image may suggest. I do believe that human and divine creativity are in some way connected and that the human imagination can indeed be a vehicle for divine revelation. Green's book helps us see, however, that such a connectedness in the imagination is qualified with the reminder of Barth's *Nein!* in his dialogue with Brunner: "no," to any suggestion of a "natural" point of contact, ontological connection or human faculty untouched by our brokenness.

He claims imagination as a *locus,* a place rather than a human faculty or possession. It is *where* revelation takes place— somewhere in the territory between human being and God, clearly uncontrolled by women and men, perhaps in the middle of our pyramid. The images I have used, pyramid and brackets, are optimistic only about human possibility, not human capacity.

Possibly I have emphasized the importance of the concept of *pastoral* beyond what is necessary for the major argument of the book. For most of my ministry I have been a practitioner, not a professor. I believe that being responsible for and to persons as their pastor or therapist is something clearly different from theorizing about it when the value of one's ministry does not rest primarily on action or consequences. Moreover, I continue to affirm that the key factor in all of this is not ordination but accountability for what one is doing in ministry to the community that authorizes it and to the person or persons being ministered to. The accountability that is associated with pastoral action is a major energizer and dynamic of pastoral theology and, perhaps, that conviction cannot be overemphasized. Special knowledge comes from doing it and learning from having done it.

Perhaps I have also overemphasized my argument with the image of the pastor as interpreter or hermeneut. Somehow this view of ministry is too "wordy"—seemingly too dependent on saying the right thing. There are too many times, as Julie's story suggests to us, when one cannot "tell someone about Jesus." At those times, however, that same person may be able to sing "Jesus Loves *You*" or commune with another by eating ice cream. I doubt that in my thinking I can escape the hermeneutical circle, but with my action and relationships, along with my interpretation of meaning, I believe I can escape. The simplicity of Macmurray's thesis seems to be a dynamic for practical theology: "All meaningful knowledge is for the sake of action, and all meaningful action for the sake of friendship." Or as I said early in the book, this kind of pastoral theology moves from something to something, from the practice of ministry to the construction or reconstruction of Christian theology. It also moves back again to ministry—where it began.

Thus the book closes with another pastoral event and some reflections that were stirred in me and in the group that first heard it. In many ways it is another unremarkable event involving a young minister and an older woman. (In my experience as a pastoral supervisor the ministry of older people to young ministers of both sexes is immense.) In the spirit of James Whitehead's "practical play of theology," I have enjoyed calling this one "Hail to Three Marys."[3]

The first Mary is our student chaplain, who relates the story of a visit with a ninety-one-year-old patient, Mary Ellen, whom she describes as "a deeply religious woman who feels angry at herself for complaining or being unhappy." "I sometimes find her helpless and demanding. . . . At other times she is a grand old lady whom I deeply admire." As the pastoral visit proceeds Chaplain Mary asks Mary Ellen, "What can I do for you today?"

Mary Ellen: Say some prayers.

Mary: What will we pray about?

Mary Ellen: You're Presbyterian, aren't you?

Mary: Yes. What is your church? I know you're Presbyterian, too.

Then there is that seemingly irrelevant discussion of churches and ministers and who was and wasn't a good minister that so often occurs in visits by chaplains. This is fortuitously interrupted as the ice cream cart is heard down the hall. (Many of us could appropriately pray for the ice cream cart to save us from irrelevance in our ministry.) Mary Ellen asks Chaplain Mary to bring her some. She does, but to Mary Ellen's consternation, she gets none for herself.

Mary Ellen: Where is your ice cream, Mary?

Mary: After I got yours, I went to get stamps for another patient, and when I came back the cart was gone.

Mary Ellen: Oh no, look at me! This is terrible!

Mary: No. Don't feel terrible. I just had lunch. You must not feel bad.

Mary Ellen: I did too, but I had ice cream also.

Notice the simplicity of this conversation, and yet one can feel that in spite of that there is something significant going on. The conversation then moves to a discussion of Mary's preparation for ministry among the "dedicated people" at the seminary.

Mary Ellen: Dedicated and well-informed. Oh, dear, I feel so ashamed. I keep thinking about the ice cream.

Mary: (somewhat impatiently) But it was not your fault. The cart was gone.

Mary Ellen: (not to be deterred) Where did it go? (After a brief discussion of that, Mary Ellen says,) You are one of God's own people.

Mary: But if God's own people don't condemn you, why do you condemn yourself? (Chaplain Mary then notes with some irritation that "there was more palaver about what a fine minister I would be, and then I said,") I have to go now, but you said you wanted prayers. What would you like me to pray about?

Mary Ellen: Well, I don't mind dying after I am dead and I go over to the other side . . . but what I fear is the process, the struggle. I don't mind dying at home, but I don't want . . .

Mary: To die in this place.

Mary Ellen: I shouldn't have said that. It is the will of God.

Mary: What is the will of God?

Mary Ellen: We must accept that God's will will be done.

Mary: (She seemed very distressed, deeply wanting to be obedient, equally deeply wanting to struggle with what appeared to her to be God's will. I did not wish to upset her faith since I had no faith with which to replace it. It seemed best just to hear her struggle, so I asked,) How can I pray about this for you, Mary Ellen?

Mary Ellen: Pray that in all circumstances I will be utterly content, secure in God's will. . . . Yes, content to be in God's will. (And then, guiltily,) Did you know that I pray the "Hail Mary" prayer sometimes? (And her Presbyterian conscience asks,) Do you think that's Mary-worship?

Mary: No I don't. In fact, I'm proud of you. It's not Mary-worship. Tell me, how does it go?

Mary Ellen: "Hail Mary, full of grace, the Lord is with thee. Blessed art thou among women, and blessed is the fruit of thy womb, Jesus. Holy Mary, Mother of God, pray for us sinners now and at the hour of our death. Amen." Do you think that sounds like Mary-worship?

Mary: No, I do not.

Mary Ellen: They say that Mary is not the mother of God, but Jesus is one of the three . . .

Mary: The Trinity . . .

Mary Ellen: And she is his mother, so she *is* the mother of God.

Mary: I think it is a beautiful prayer.

Mary Ellen: When you pray you must ask for me to be forgiven for my sins.

Mary: (prays as she is asked, after which Mary Ellen prays for her and her work) Mary Ellen, you are a kind and good lady.

Mary Ellen: I have fooled you then. (meaning she is not kind and good)

Mary: (laughs, but then realizes that Mary Ellen is quite serious)

Mary Ellen: Now Mary, you be good.

Mary: I will be good, but I will be bad sometimes, too. (She looked a little startled, but I thought she could handle it.) Now, good-bye and thank you. (Chaplain Mary leans over and kisses Mary Ellen on the forehead, covers her feet and leaves the room.)

This is a routine visit to a ninety-one-year-old woman on an ordinary day, yet the symbols that emerge in the conversation between the two Marys, as Tillich instructed us, "point beyond themselves." To me they seem almost inexhaustible: two Marys struggling over their identity as children of God, their likeness to and differences from each other, their goodness and badness, and their venture into an encounter with the mysterious third Mary so full of grace and who, perhaps even for Presbyterians will "pray for us sinners now and at the hour of our death." In this fascinating mix of simplicity and profundity is an affirmation by the Marys of a God who may be interested not just in goodness, but in our struggle between goodness and badness and our efforts to discover—even in the tenth decade—just who we really are.

The pastoral event seems to reach toward and push against the theological roots of our pastoral ministry. It opposes and fights with, not only the Sunday school God of insipid goodness, but also that masculine, Presbyterian God who seems to be fearful of the third Mary. Pastoral theology at its best helps us to recover our heritage, and to recover from it. Wesley, Calvin, Luther, and even Acquinas may be able to bring one Mary into theological line, but probably not two, and certainly not three Marys.

I think these reflections are what James Whitehead meant by theological play or testing the leeway. Like two centers in basketball, pushing against each other to gain position, the theology that grows out of the events of ministry is a contact sport in which there will inevitably be fouls called (sometimes by referees who never played the game very well themselves). But a good game of theology always involves strong opposition and contact under the basket.

Thinking Theologically About Pastoral Events

The first step in thinking theologically about pastoral events is developing a climate and community in which theological thinking and sharing can take place. There are various ways of doing this. One way includes sharing stories. Stories can be told without writing them, but the advantage of writing is objectifying the story and, in effect, giving it away to others: on one hand taking one's story seriously enough to write it and on the other giving it away by putting it in a particular form. That form enables others to take it without continuing to depend on the original storyteller. The other element in developing a facilitating climate and a community is requiring that stories and events be reacted to personally rather than criticized according to the usual standards for writing. One never fully escapes the critical response, but attempting at first to bracket out criticism allows the writer to risk using his or her imagination with some confidence that this will be accepted.

The second step is taking one's willingness to "play" with one's story *through* the imagination into the theological arena. Since there is a strong element of something received or given in all theology, there are a number of rules for playing the theological game. One must have a sense that one's family theology and what one learned as the church's beliefs are okay. At the same time having a sense of one's own separate and distinct theological position and direction is essential. To do theology one must be in touch with both *our* story of one's religious community and the unique *my* story of faith. Another important rule has to do with the building blocks of theology or theological method, learning something of how others have made theological arguments. One's own argument does not have to be the same, but it does have to have some similarities in order to be judged to communicate effectively in the theological arena.

The third step is looking at one's clinical or pastoral experience by using the wisdom of one's theological heritage along with one's imagination and making a judgment about what events are "meaning-full" and thus demanding theological exploration. The criteria for making this judgment are more intuitive and imaginative than objective. There is a sense of transcendence of the immediate case material and claim of general relevance. "This person is expressing the human situation, the relation of persons to each other, the world, or to God." The uniqueness of the situation informs what we already know or believe. "What is expressed here in a unique way really has something to say to all of us."

Structure and Agenda For Ministry Groups

Show and Tell for Adults—
How Group Members Capture Their Experiencing

First session: Introduction to the value of capturing one's experience and a method of sharing and responding to it.

Second session: Sharing and responding to events from the everyday experience of group members.

Third session: Sharing and responding to events from the past, usually the description of an event from late childhood or early adolescence in order to get a pre-adult look at the world.

Fourth session: Sharing and responding to sacred places and things from the past, for example, a description of a home we lived in, a neighborhood, a special place in the home, or a symbolic object representative of an important part of our life.

Fifth session: Sharing and responding to imagined events from the future. Group members write about an event that takes place five years from now.

Events Revealing Our Relationship to Communities of Origin

Sixth session: Sharing and responding to myths and parables. Using the definition that myth is a story that creates or forms a way of explaining the particular world we live in, and parable is a story that destroys or undercuts one's way of looking at the world, the group members write and share myths and parables.

Seventh session: Sharing and responding to events that reveal how we are formed by and are differentiating ourselves from our families of origin.

Eighth session: Sharing and responding to how we are a part of a particular religious tradition but also differentiated from it—our theology and my theology.

Theological Reflection on Pastoral Events

Ninth session: Sharing and responding to events that reveal the character of our ministry and contribute to what we understand ministry to be.

Tenth session: Sharing and responding to pastoral events that are "meaning-full" and that may change or enrich our understanding of theological concepts other than ministry.

Eleventh session: Theological consultation on how particular pastoral events may "talk back" to and enrich theology.

Twelfth session: Sharing theological formulations growing out of pastoral events.

Notes

Prologue

1. John Patton, "Toward a Theology of Pastoral Event: Reflections on the Work of Seward Hiltner," *The Journal of Pastoral Care* 40 (June 1986): 131.
2. James D. Whitehead and Evelyn Eaton Whitehead, *Method in Ministry: Theological Reflection and Christian Ministry* (New York: The Seabury Press, 1981).
3. Ernest G. Schactel, "On Memory and Childhood Amnesia," *A Study of Interpersonal Relations,* Patrick Mullahy, ed. (New York: Hermitage Press, 1949), p. 12.
4. William James, *The Varieties of Religious Experience* (New York: The New American Library, 1958), p. 26.
5. Seward Hiltner, *Preface to Pastoral Theology* (Nashville: Abingdon Press, 1958), p. 23.
6. Don S. Browning, *Religious Ethics and Pastoral Care* (Philadelphia: Fortress Press, 1983), p. 16. Interestingly, Browning has used William James's concern for the moral life as an important element in developing his point of view. I focus more on a different element in James to develop an alternate position.
7. Charles V. Gerkin, *The Living Human Document* (Nashville: Abingdon Press, 1984); Charles Winquist, *Practical Hermeneutics* (Chico, Calif.: Scholars Press, 1980); Donald Capps, *Pastoral Care and Hermeneutics* (Philadelphia: Fortress Press, 1984).
8. Robert W. Funk, *Language, Hermeneutic, and Word of God* (New York: Harper & Row, 1966).
9. Karl Menninger, *Theory of Psychoanalytic Technique* (New York: Basic Books, 1958), p. 129.
10. James N. Poling and Donald E. Miller, *Foundations for a Practical Theology of Ministry* (Nashville: Abingdon, 1985), pp. 64-65.
11. Theodore W. Jennings, Jr., *Introduction to Theology* (Philadelphia: Fortress Press, 1976), p. 17.

1. Event and Imagination

1. Sigmund Freud, "Recommendations for Physicians on the Psycho-Analytic Method of Treatment (1912)," *Collected Papers*, vol. II (London: The Hogarth Press, 1953), pp. 326-27. I became reacquainted with this paper of Freud's through reading a recent book by Alfred Margulies, *The Empathic Imagination* (New York: W. W. Norton, 1989).

2. Carl R. Rogers, "Persons or Science? A Philosophical Question," *On Becoming a Person* (Boston: Houghton Mifflin Co., 1961), pp. 199-224.

3. Daniel Day Williams, "Suffering and Being in Empirical Theology," *The Future of Empirical Theology*, Bernard E. Meland, ed. (Chicago: The University of Chicago Press, 1969), p. 176.

4. Ross Snyder, *Contemporary Celebration* (Nashville: Abingdon Press, 1971), particularly chapter 6.

5. William James, *The Varieties of Religious Experience* (New York: New American Library, 1958).

6. James M. Edie, *William James and Phenomenology* (Bloomington/Indianapolis: Indiana University Press, 1987), p. 47.

7. William James, *The Principles of Psychology*, vol. II (New York: Henry Holt Co., 1902), p. 293.

8. Edie, *William James*, p. 5.

9. Ibid., p. 33.

10. William James, *The Writings of William James: A Comprehensive Edition*, John J. McDermott, ed. (Chicago: University of Chicago Press), p. 215.

11. James, *Principles of Psychology*, vol. I, chapter 10.

12. Edie, *William James*, p. 73.

13. Laura N. Rice and Leslie S. Greenberg, eds., *Patterns of Change: Intensive Analysis of Psychotherapeutic Process* (New York: The Guilford Press, 1984), pp. vi, 11.

14. Laura N. Rice and Eva Pila Saperia, "Task Analysis of the Resolution of Problematic Reactions," *Patterns of Change*, pp. 33-34.

15. Ibid., pp. 34-35.

16. Ibid., pp. 40-41.

17. Robert Elliott, "A Discovery-Oriented Approach to Significant Change Events in Psychotherapy: Interpersonal Process Recall and Comprehensive Process Analysis," *Patterns of Change*, p. 253.

18. Margulies, *Empathic Imagination*, p. 5.

19. Ibid., pp. 7 and 8.

20. Ibid., p. 12.

21. Ibid., pp. 14-15.

22. Ibid., p. 15.

23. Paul T. Brockelman, *Existential Phenomenology and the World of Ordinary Experience: An Introduction* (Washington, D.C.: University Press of America, 1980), pp. 55-56.

24. Maurice Merleau-Pointy, *Phenomenology of Perception* (London: Routledge & Kegan Paul, 1962), p. x.

25. Brockelman, *Existential Phenomenology*, p. 59.

26. Ibid., p. 61.

27. Ibid., p. 67.

28. Merleau-Ponty, *The Primacy of Perception* (Northwestern University Press, 1964).

29. Brockelman, *Existential Phenomenology,* pp. 64-65.

30. Eugene T. Gendlin, "Experiential Psychotherapy," *Current Psychotherapies,* Raymond Corsini, ed. (Itasco, Ill.: Peacock, 1973), p. 322.

31. Gendlin, "Experience, A Variable in the Process of Therapeutic Change," *The American Journal of Psychotherapy* 15 (April 1961): 237.

32. See Gendlin, *Focusing* (New York: Bantam Books, 1981), parts I and II.

33. Gendlin, "The Role of Knowledge in Practice," *The Counselor's Handbook,* ed. Gail F. Farwell, Neal R. Gamsky, and Philippa Mathieu-Coughlon, (New York: Intext Educational Publishers, 1974), p. 284.

34. Gendlin, "Experiential Psychotherapy," p. 324.

35. Gendlin, *Experiencing and the Creation of Meaning* (New York: The Free Press, 1962), p. 38.

36. John M. Schlien, "Phenomenology and Personality," *Concepts of Personality,* Joseph M. Wepman and Ralph W. Heine, eds. (Chicago: Aldine Publishing, 1963), pp. 324-25.

37. Edward Farley, *Ecclesial Man* (Philadelphia: Fortress Press, 1975), pp. 71, 72.

38. Ibid., p. 77.

39. Ibid., p. 81.

40. Michael Polanyi, as quoted in Farley, *Ecclesial Man,* p. 106.

41. John Patton, "The 'Secret' of Pastoral Counseling," *The Journal of Pastoral Care* 36 (June 1982): 73-75.

42. Paul W. Pruyser, "A Transformational Understanding of Humanity," *Changing Views of the Human Condition,* Paul W. Pruyser, ed. (Macon, Ga.: Mercer University Press, 1987), p. 5.

2. Ministry and Community

1. Victor Turner, *The Ritual Process* (Ithaca, N.Y.: Cornell University Press, 1977), pp. 96-97.

2. Ibid., p. 127.

3. Maurice Merleau-Ponty, *The Phenomenology of Perception,* p. 168, as quoted in Edward Farley, *Ecclesial Man* (Philadelphia: Fortress Press, 1975), p. 77.

4. Edward Farley, *Ecclesial Reflection: An Anatomy of Theological Method* (Philadelphia: Fortress Press, 1982), note 5 on p. 199.

5. John Patton, *Is Human Forgiveness Possible?* (Nashville: Abingdon Press, 1985).

6. Farley, *Ecclesial Man,* pp. 93-98. See also the understanding of *"special relations"* in Patton, *Is Human Forgiveness Possible?*

7. Farley, *Ecclesial Man,* p. 107

8. Frank G. Kirkpatrick, *Community: A Trinity of Models* (Washington, D.C.: Georgetown University Press, 1986).

9. John Macmurray, *The Self As Agent* (New York: Harper & Brothers, 1961), p. 16.

10. Ibid., p. 31.

11. Ibid., pp. 25-26.

12. John Macmurray, *Persons in Relation* (New York: Harper & Brothers, 1961), pp. 76-77.

13. Macmurray, *Agent,* p. 86.

14. Ibid., p. 116.

15. Macmurray, *Persons,* pp. 60-61.

16. Ibid., p. 63.

17. Ibid., pp. 70-71.

18. Ibid., pp. 157-58.

19. Paul Tillich, "The Theology of Pastoral Care," *Pastoral Psychology* 10 (October 1959): 21-26.

20. John Patton and Brian H. Childs, *Christian Marriage and Family: Caring for Your Generations* (Nashville: Abingdon Press, 1988), pp. 227-28.

21. Edward Farley, *Theologia: The Fragmentation and Unity of Theological Education* (Philadelphia: Fortress Press, 1983), p. 115.

22. Ibid., p. 176.

23. Ibid., p. 153.

24. Jackson W. Carroll, *Theological Education* 21, (Spring 1985): 31. See also, Carroll, *Ministry as Reflective Practice: A New Look at the Professional Model* (Washington, D.C.: The Alban Institute, 1986); Donald A. Schoen, *The Reflective Practitioner: How Professionals Think in Action* (New York: Basic Books Publishers, 1983); and Schoen, *Educating the Reflective Practitioner: Toward a New Design for Teaching and Learning in the Professions* (San Francisco: Jossey-Bass, 1987).

25. James M. Gustafson, "Professions as 'Callings,'" *Social Service Review* (December 1982): 514.

26. Paul W. Pruyser, *Changing Views of the Human Condition* (Macon, Ga.: Mercer University Press, 1987), p. 5.

27. Ibid., p. 7.

28. Stanley Hauerwas and William H. Willimon, "Ministry as More than a Helping Profession," *The Christian Century* 106 (March 15, 1989): 282-84. See also William L. Sachs, "Willimon's Project: Does It Make Sense?" *The Christian Century* 106, no. 13: 412-14.

29. John Patton, "A Theological Interpretation of Pastoral Supervision," *The New Shape of Pastoral Theology* (New York/Nashville: Abingdon Press, 1969), pp. 241-42.

30. John D. Caputo, *Radical Hermeneutics: Repetition, Deconstruction, and the Hermeneutic Project* (Bloomington and Indianapolis: Indiana University Press, 1987).

31. Ibid., pp. 5-6.

32. Rodney J. Hunter, "The Future of Pastoral Theology," *Pastoral Psychology* 29 (Fall 1980): 58-69 and in an unpublished paper dated April 19, 1989.

33. Hunter, unpublished paper.

34. Paul Ramsey, "Liturgy and Ethics," *Journal of Religious Ethics* 7 (1979): 139-71.

35. Ibid., p. 6.

36. Ronald L. Grimes, "Of Words the Speaker, Of Deeds the Doer," *The Journal of Religion* 66 (January 1986): 5.

37. Ibid., p. 6.

38. John Patton, "Ministry in Extended Care Facilities," *Pastor and Patient: a Handbook for Clergy Who Visit the Sick,* Richard Dayringer, ed. (New York: Jason Aronson, 1982), pp. 260-61. This story was originally presented in a part-time clinical course in pastoral care many years ago.

39. John Patton, "The Myth of Itineracy," *Circuit Rider* 5 (September 1981): 3-4.

3. Action and Interpretation

1. Seward Hiltner, *Preface to Pastoral Theology* (Nashville: Abingdon Press, 1958), chapter 7.

2. Edward Farley, *Ecclesial Man* (Philadelphia: Fortress Press, 1979), p. 70.

3. Farley, *Ecclesial Reflection* (Philadelphia: Fortress Press, 1962), pp. 176-77.

4. Ibid., p. 183.

5. Ibid., p. 187.

6. Leslie Stevenson, *Seven Theories of Human Nature* (New York: Oxford University Press, 1987); Paul Pruyser, ed., *Changing View of the Human Condition* (Macon, Ga.: Mercer University Press, 1987).

7. Farley, *Ecclesial Reflection,* p. 189.

8. Ibid., p. 196.

9. Ibid.

10. Nancy Frankenberry, *Religion and Radical Empiricism* (Albany: State University of New York Press, 1987), p. 144.

11. Ibid., p. 187.

12. Paul Ricoeur, *Interpretation Theory: Discourse and the Surplus of Meaning* (Fort Worth: The Texas Christian University Press, 1976), pp. 20-21.

13. Ibid., pp. 59-69.

14. Bernard E. Meland, *Fallible Forms and Symbols* (Philadelphia: Fortress Press, 1976), p. viii.

15. Meland, "Grace: A Dimension of Nature?" *The Journal of Religion* 54, no. 2 (April 1974): 136-37.

16. James N. Poling and Donald E. Miller, *Foundations for a Practical Theology of Ministry* (Nashville: Abingdon Press, 1985), p. 68.

17. Walter Brueggemann, *The Message of the Psalms: A Theological Commentary* (Minneapolis: Augsburg Publishing House, 1984).

18. Gordon D. Kaufman, *An Essay on Theological Method* (Chico, Calif.: The Scholars Press, 1975).

19. James D. Whitehead, "The Practical Play of Theology," *The Promise of Practical Theology: Formation and Reflection,* Lewis S. Mudge and James N. Poling, eds. (Philadelphia: Fortress Press, 1987), pp. 39-40.

20. Ibid., p. 44.

21. Ibid., p. 48.

22. Ibid., p. 50.

23. Anne Carr, "Theology and Experience in the Thought of Karl Rahner," *The Journal of Religion* 53 (July 1973): 375.

Epilogue

1. William James, "The Will to Believe," *Essays in Pragmatism* (New York: Hafner Publishing Company, 1952), p. 103.

2. Garrett Green, *Imagining God: Theology and the Religious Imagination* (San Francisco: Harper & Row, 1989), p. 4.

3. John Patton, "Pastoral Supervision and Theology," *Journal of Supervision and Training in Ministry* 8 (1986): 59-71.